Discovery EDUCATION | SOCIAL STUDIES TECHBOOK

S0-BZE-445

MEDIEVAL AND EARLY MODERN WORLD HISTORY
CALIFORNIA EDITION

**Log in to Discovery Education
Social Studies Techbook
at DiscoveryEducation.com**

ISBN 13: 978-1-68220-236-4

Printed in the United States of America.

4 5 6 7 8 9 CWR 23 22 21 20   A

800-323-9084
4350 Congress Street, Suite 700, Charlotte, NC 28209
©2017 Discovery Education. All rights reserved.

Table of Contents

CHAPTER 7 | *Early Americas*

CONCEPTS

CHAPTER 8 | *African Empires*

CONCEPTS

UNIT 3 | New Horizons, New Ideas

CHAPTER 9 | *The Renaissance*

CONCEPTS

CHAPTER 10 | *Exploration and Conquest*

CONCEPTS

CHAPTER 11 | *The Seeds of the Modern World*

CONCEPTS

Letter to the Student

Dear Student,

Welcome to World History! You're about to begin an exciting journey into the world of Social Studies. There's more to world history than you might think. In this course, you will examine the ways cultures grew, changed, and interacted with one another in the Medieval and Early Modern Eras. As the regions of the world grew more interconnected, people from around the world began to share ideas and struggle for power with each other. Then, you will use what you have learned to analyze and understand present-day issues and propose solutions.

This resource is designed to use your reading and writing skills and prepare you for college, a career, and civic life.

Each lesson in this course is called a concept. Each concept has an Essential Question to guide your investigation of the main topic. The different tabs guide you through the lesson.

- ENGAGE: What do I know about this topic? What do I want to learn? Make connections between past and present learning as you dive into the concept.

- EXPLORE: Interact with text and multimedia as you explore key people, places, and events.

- EXPLAIN: Describe what you learned about the concept's topics and submit your answers online.

- ELABORATE: Examine primary sources, analyze complex problems, and complete activities to go deeper into the concept.

- EVALUATE: Review the concept's information with flashcards, quizzes, and writing assignments that help you express your position on critical topics.

Get ready to learn about the people, places, and ideas that have shaped World History.

The Discovery Education Team

Keep this resource handy as you explore the digital Techbook:

- **FLASHCARDS** for reviewing each concept's essential information
- **GRAPHIC ORGANIZERS** for taking notes on the Core Interactive Text
- **FOCUS QUESTIONS** for working through each concept ·
- **QR CODES** for connecting to Techbook pages and activities

Discovery Education Digital Connections

 Core Interactive Text: Explore an exciting combination of videos, photographs, audio recordings, interactive maps, and activities. A variety of reading tools, including highlighting, taking notes, two different text levels, text-to-speech, and Spanish translations will help you understand the text.

 Techbook Atlas: Use this interactive map to explore the human and physical geography of Earth with different overlays and base maps.

 Reference: View the definition and related media for key words and phrases.

 Global News: Watch exclusive videos that summarize the week's most pressing global news, through a Discovery Education partnership with trusted news leader MacNeil/Lehrer Productions.

 Online Entry: Submit your answers online for EXPLAIN activities, and be sure to check the evaluation criteria or rubric before you do.

 Interactive Investigations: Found on the ELABORATE tab and other places, these activities challenge you to make critical decisions and study change over time through analyzing people, data, and places.

 Board Builder: Use images and text to create presentations with this handy tool.

UNIT 1: EMPIRE, BELIEF, AND POWER

Chapter 1: Connecting the World

1.1 The World in 300 CE

LESSON OVERVIEW

Lesson Objectives:

By the end of this lesson, you should be able to:

- **Describe the economic and cultural connections between civilizations across Afro-Eurasia.**
- **Describe the early cultures of the Americas.**
- **Analyze the continuity and change in life outside major kingdoms.**

Key Vocabulary

Aksum, Alexander the Great, Andes, aqueduct, Ashoka, Buddhism, bureaucracy, Chandragupta I, Confucianism, cultural diffusion, dynasty, Emperor Wu, empire, Gupta Empire, Han dynasty, Huns, Jainism, Liu Bang, maize, Maya, Oceania, pastoral, Persia, Roman Empire, Silk Road, steppe

Lesson Essential Question:

How did the regions of the world interact around 300 CE?

FLASHCARDS

1. The Kingdoms of Ancient Afro-Eurasia

In 300 CE, there were many large kingdoms and empires in Europe, Asia, and Africa. These kingdoms were interconnected by extensive trade routes.

- The Roman Empire dominated Europe, the Mediterranean, and North Africa. Roman rule created a common language and many common customs.

- In Asia, powerful empires such as the Parthian, Sasanian, Gupta, and Han dynasty ruled. These empires valued art and learning and encouraged the flourishing of vibrant cultures. They produced luxury goods that the West sought.

- The trade among the large kingdoms allowed smaller kingdoms to develop in East Africa, Southeast Asia, and Arabia. These kingdoms earned their wealth through trade and served as intermediaries in the economy of the ancient world.

- By 200 CE, traders traveled well-developed trade routes, passing luxury goods between the empires. Along with these goods, people exchanged ideas, beliefs, and even diseases.

Why Does It Matter?

The vibrant trade between the kingdoms of the ancient world led to innovation and the development of philosophy, science, math, literature, and art across Europe, Asia, and Africa.

photo: The J. Paul Getty Museum

This is a glass kohl holder from the Roman Empire. Kohl was a popular eye makeup in the Roman Empire. The practice of using kohl was popular in ancient Egypt. Glassblowing originated in Southwest Asia.

2. The Ancient Americas

Around 200 CE, major civilizations arose in Mesoamerica and the Andes Mountains.

- For each of the cultures, the development of advanced agricultural techniques like chinampas, raised beds, canals, and aqueducts created a stable food base, allowing the populations to flourish.

- Cities like Teotihuacan and Tiwanaku thrived on extensive trade over large areas. As a result, their beliefs, ideas, and symbols spread widely.

- In each of the civilizations, art and religion played an important role, with each building massive pyramids and temples and adorning them with scenes of religious rituals and depictions of the gods. Some of the clearest examples of this come from the Mayan culture.

- In Moche and other civilizations, art and crafts like pottery, metalworking, and textiles are evidence of advanced cultures. They also helped foster trade between regions.

- The Maya made major advances in science and mathematics, including development of a calendar and precise astronomy.

Why Does It Matter?

The civilizations of the ancient Americas were connected through trade and shared ideas and beliefs. As a result, each culture enriched the others, allowing for the development of complex civilizations.

photo: Pixabay

Teotihuacan was one of the largest cities in the world in 300 CE. The agricultural innovations, religious practices, and political organization of Teotihuacan would influence later civilizations in the region.

FLASHCARDS

3 ▶ Life Outside the Kingdoms

While many people lived within the borders of the great kingdoms of the ancient world, many more lived outside them.

- Nomads lived off the goats and sheep they herded across the grasslands, as well as raids on the settlements within their reach. They developed many innovations that were incorporated into the kingdoms.

- Other groups established more permanent settlements, but they were pushed or pulled to continually migrate, either by a lack of resources or a desire to explore.

- Hunter-gatherers lived off the land, hunting game and foraging for plants, berries, and nuts. They were usually mobile over a large area, but they sometimes settled when they found an area with an abundance of food.

Why Does It Matter?

Although they lived in different ways and had different traditions, all of the societies outside the kingdoms were mobile to some degree, allowing them to develop complex cultures that incorporated new ideas and influenced the cultures of the kingdoms.

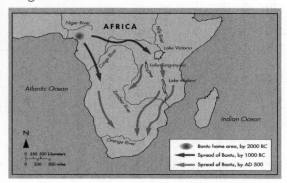

photo: Discovery Education

The Bantu migration spread new people, languages, cultures, and even economic models to Central and South Africa.

Name _____ Date _____

GRAPHIC ORGANIZER: Comparison Chart

Use this Comparison Chart to summarize and record details about the empires that existed around 300 CE. For supporting resources, go to Empire, Belief, and Power > Connecting the World > The World in 300 CE > Explore > Empires Connect Regions.

Empire	Reign	Art and Science	Trade	Reasons for Decline
Roman Empire				
Parthian Empire				
Sasanian Empire				
Gupta Empire				

Name _____ Date _____

GRAPHIC ORGANIZER: Comparison Chart *(continued)*

Empire	Reign	Art and Science	Trade	Reasons for Decline
Han Dynasty				
Teotihuacan				
Maya Empire				
Tiwanaku				
Moche				

Name _____ **Date** _____

GRAPHIC ORGANIZER: Summary Frames

Use these Summary Frames to sketch a drawing that summarizes the information under each heading in the Core Interactive Text. Include a caption that describes what you drew. For supporting resources, go to Empire, Belief, and Power > Connecting the World > The World in 300 CE > Explore > Kingdoms of Trade.

East Africa	Southeast Asia	Arabia

_____   _____   _____

_____   _____   _____

_____   _____   _____

Persian Royal Road	Many Trade Routes in One	Ideas Travel with Trade

_____   _____   _____

_____   _____   _____

_____   _____   _____

Name _____ Date _____

GRAPHIC ORGANIZER: Main Idea Web

Use this Main Idea Web to organize details related to migrating peoples of 300 CE. For supporting resources, go to Empire, Belief, and Power > Connecting the World > The World in 300 CE > Explore > People on the Move.

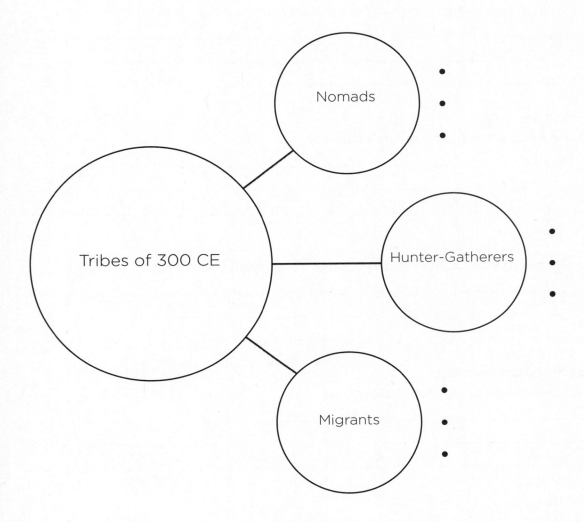

Tribes of 300 CE

Nomads
-
-
-

Hunter-Gatherers
-
-
-

Migrants
-
-
-

Name _____ **Date** _____

EXPLORE: FOCUS QUESTIONS

Using what you learned from the Core Interactive Text, answer each page's focus question:

Empires Connect Regions

How did large empires create cultural unity and encourage cultural diffusion across regions?

_____
_____
_____

The Persian Empires

How did the Persian empires shape the region's culture?

_____
_____
_____

Empire in India

How did the Indian economy and culture flourish during the Gupta Empire?

_____
_____
_____

The Han Dynasty Unites the East

What were the cultural values of the Han dynasty?

_____
_____
_____

Kingdoms of Trade

What role did trade play in the development of smaller kingdoms throughout the Middle East, Africa, and Asia?

_____
_____
_____

The Silk Road

How did the Silk Road foster connections between ancient civilizations?

_____
_____
_____

Name _____ Date _____

EXPLORE: FOCUS QUESTIONS *(continued)*

A Pre-Columbian Metropolis
How did Teotihuacan shape the culture of Mesoamerica?

_____

_____

_____

Central and South America
How did the environment shape the American cultures?

_____

_____

_____

People on the Move
How did nomadic groups help spread ideas throughout Asia and Africa?

_____

_____

_____

Migrations
How did migrations impact populations around the world?

_____

_____

_____

PROJECTS AND ASSESSMENTS

Explain Activities

ACTIVITY TYPE: ADVERTISEMENT

Travel the World

In this activity, you will create a tourism brochure for an ancient empire.

ACTIVITY TYPE: QUICK WRITE

Local or Global?

In this activity, you will evaluate the interconnectedness of cultures in 300 CE by responding to the prompt: To what extent were cultures "global" or "local" around 300 CE?

ACTIVITY TYPE: SOCIAL STUDIES EXPLANATION

The World in 300 CE

In this Social Studies Explanation activity, you will use a template to assemble evidence from the sources you have explored. Then, you will write an answer to the Essential Question and defend your answer with supporting evidence.

Elaborate Activities

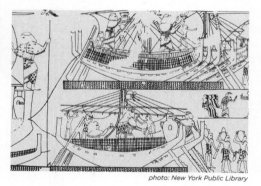

photo: New York Public Library

ACTIVITY TYPE: ROLE PLAY

Building a Trade Empire

In this activity, you will create a presentation for the queen of a small but wealthy city-state in Southwest Asia circa 200 CE about the benefits and costs of creating trade and cultural ties with another kingdom.

photo: Library of Congress

ACTIVITY TYPE: SOCRATIC SEMINAR

A Trader's Guide to the Red Sea

In this activity, you will read excerpts from the *Periplus of the Erythraean Sea*, view a video about globalization, and complete a discussion about these sources.

Evaluate Activities

BRIEF-CONSTRUCTED RESPONSE (BCR)

Sharing Ideas

EXTENDED-CONSTRUCTED RESPONSE (ECR)

A Chinese View of Rome

photo: Getty Images

UNIT 1: EMPIRE, BELIEF, AND POWER

Chapter 2: The Roman Republic and Empire

2.1 Geography and Economy of Ancient Rome

LESSON OVERVIEW

Lesson Objectives:

By the end of this lesson, you should be able to:

- **Locate ancient Rome and its important cities and rivers on a historical and a modern map.**
- **Connect ancient Rome's location and its expansion through conquest and trade.**
- **Analyze the impact of coined money and roads on trade inside the Roman Empire.**

Key Vocabulary

Aachen, agriculture, Alps, Apennine Mountains, barter, climate, climate region, ecosystem, empire, Forum, Gaul, George Washington, Great Britain, Italy, latitude, Latium, longitude, markets, Mediterranean Sea, North Africa, peninsula, Remus, Roman Empire, Rome, Romulus, Spain, Tiber River

Lesson Essential Question:

How did geography and trade routes impact the growth of Rome?

FLASHCARDS

1 Where Was Rome?

Rome grew from a city in central Italy to a huge empire that occupied parts of Europe, Africa, and Asia all at once.

- **Rome was founded on the Tiber River, in the center of the Italian peninsula.**
- **The Roman Empire expanded as far north as modern-day Great Britain and Scotland.**
- **The empire expanded as far southwest as the country of Morocco and as far east as the country of Syria.**

Why Does It Matter?

The location of Rome led to the success of the city and its eventual expansion into an empire. Rome's large size meant that it had a significant influence through its military, trade, and culture.

photo: Corbis

The Roman Empire began as a small city in central Italy but expanded greatly over hundreds of years.

2 Location Leads to Expansion

Rome's location and geography gave it advantages that other locations did not have.

- **Rome's location on the Tiber River in central Italy meant that Roman traders could easily sail the Mediterranean to trade with other places.**
- **The mountains and hills of Italy helped keep Romans safe from invasions.**
- **Rome's warm climate meant that it was a good location for farming, which meant that Romans had a plentiful food supply.**

Why Does It Matter?

Rome's geographic conditions helped it to develop a trade-based economy and made it easier for Rome to expand throughout the Mediterranean region.

photo: Library of Congress

Rome's location and climate made it an excellent location for growing grains and other crops.

FLASHCARDS *(continued)*

3 **Roman Roads and Coins**

Roman coins and roads helped make trade and travel much easier during the Roman Empire.

- Romans built thousands of miles of roads and bridges that were used by soldiers, messengers, and traders throughout the empire.
- Romans had such advanced engineering technology that some of their roads still exist today.
- Romans minted coins that were used for trade throughout the empire and showed images of Roman rulers, gods, and goddesses.

Why Does It Matter?

Accomplishments such as roads, bridges, and coins helped Romans develop trade networks that allowed them to prosper and helped unify the empire.

photo: Library of Congress

The development of roads made travel and trade throughout the empire easier. This helped Rome expand its influence and empire.

Name _____ **Date** _____

GRAPHIC ORGANIZER: Main Idea Web

Use this Main Idea Web to organize details about the geography of Rome. For supporting resources, go to Empire, Belief, and Power > The Roman Republic and Empire > Geography and Economy of Ancient Rome > Explore > The Founding of Rome.

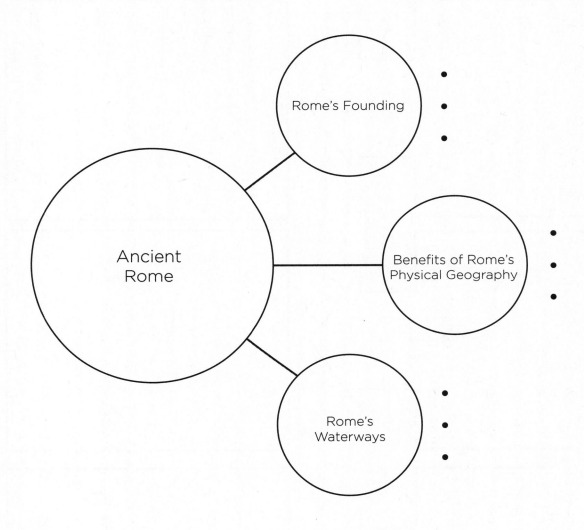

Name _____ **Date** _____

GRAPHIC ORGANIZER: Problem/Solution Chart

Use this Problem/Solution Chart to describe the challenges that Rome faced as it expanded its territory (problems) and the ways in which Roman citizens met those challenges (solutions). For supporting resources, go to Empire, Belief, and Power > The Roman Republic and Empire > Geography and Economy of Ancient Rome > Explore > Roman Roads and Bridges.

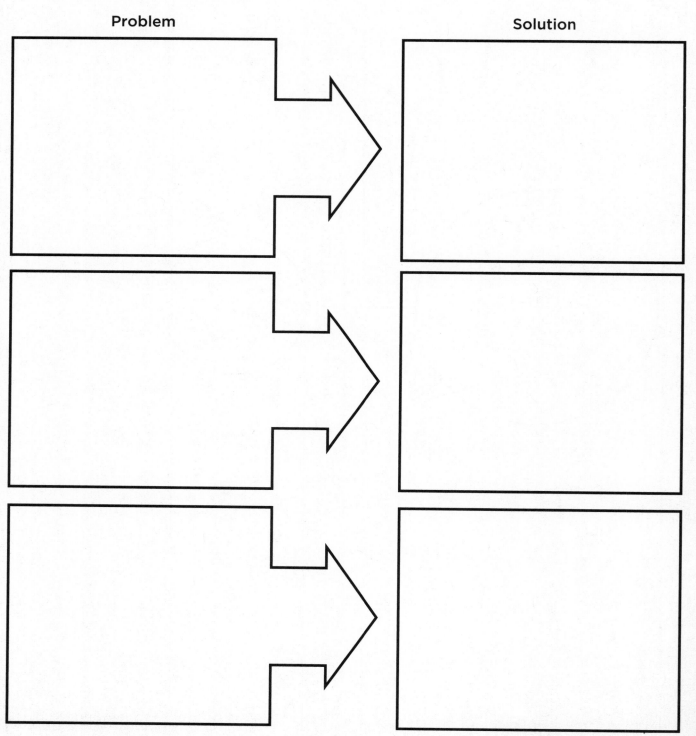

Problem   **Solution**

Name _____ Date _____

GRAPHIC ORGANIZER: Problem/Solution Chart *(continued)*

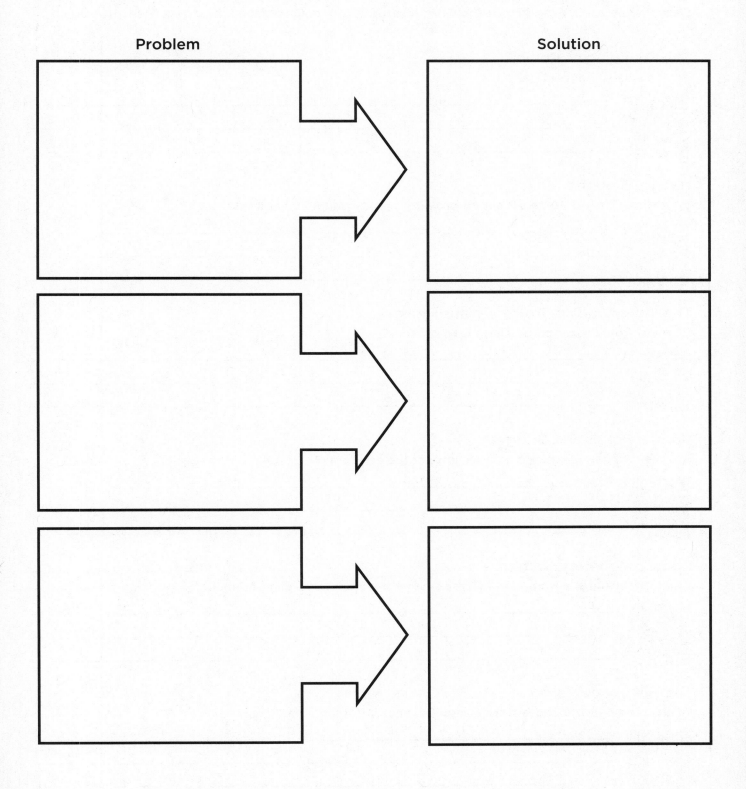

Problem   Solution

Name _____ Date _____

EXPLORE: FOCUS QUESTIONS

Using what you learned from the Core Interactive Text, answer each page's focus question:

The Founding of Rome
Where was ancient Rome?

_____

_____

_____

Natural Benefits
What benefits did Rome's location provide the city and its inhabitants?

_____

_____

_____

The Importance of Rome's Waterways
How did Rome's geography help it to prosper?

_____

_____

_____

Roman Roads and Bridges
How did Roman roads and bridges impact the economy?

_____

_____

_____

Rome's Monetary System
What effect did the Roman monetary system have on Rome's economy?

_____

_____

_____

The History of Money
What is the cultural and historical significance of Roman coins?

_____

_____

_____

PROJECTS AND ASSESSMENTS

Explain Activities

ACTIVITY TYPE: DIAGRAM

Geography and Economy of Rome

Use at least 10 words from the Word Bank to create a graphic response to the Essential Question.

ACTIVITY TYPE: ADVERTISEMENT

Roman Innovations

In this activity, you will create an advertisement for a company that has created a new innovation related to Roman roads or coins.

ACTIVITY TYPE: SOCIAL STUDIES EXPLANATION

Geography and Economy of Ancient Rome

In this Social Studies Explanation activity, you will use a template to assemble evidence from the sources you have explored. Then, you will write an answer to the Essential Question and defend your answer with supporting evidence.

Elaborate Activities

photo: Getty Images

INVESTIGATION TYPE: DATA ANALYSIS

Transportation and Trade in Ancient Rome

Your mission is to analyze the methods of transportation and trade routes used by the Romans as their empire expanded to the edges of the known world.

photo: Library of Congress

ACTIVITY TYPE: SAY WHAT?

Rome and Its Surroundings

In this activity, you will read one excerpt from either Strabo's "Geographica" or Titus Livius's "The History of Rome" and translate it for modern times.

PROJECTS AND ASSESSMENTS *(continued)*

photo: Getty Images

ACTIVITY TYPE: CURRENT EVENTS CONNECTION

Unification, Past and Present

In this activity, you will research how both the Roman Empire and the European Union used travel, trade, and currency to achieve unification. You will then write a speech to be given to a future world organization comparing the two unions and explaining which was more successful and why.

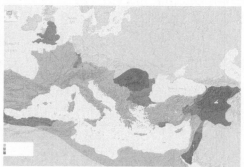

photo: Discovery Education

ACTIVITY TYPE: DOCUMENT-BASED INVESTIGATION

Rome: Geography and Economy

As the Roman Empire grew and spread through the Mediterranean and across Europe and parts of Asia, the culture of Rome diffused across the conquered territories. Military conquest, technological advancements, and trade relationships all helped foster this diffusion. In this Document-Based Investigation, you will analyze source materials and investigate this question: How did trade help spread Roman ways of life throughout the empire?

Evaluate Activities

BRIEF-CONSTRUCTED RESPONSE (BCR)

Geography and Economy of Ancient Rome

EXTENDED-CONSTRUCTED RESPONSE (ECR)

Geography and Economy of Ancient Rome

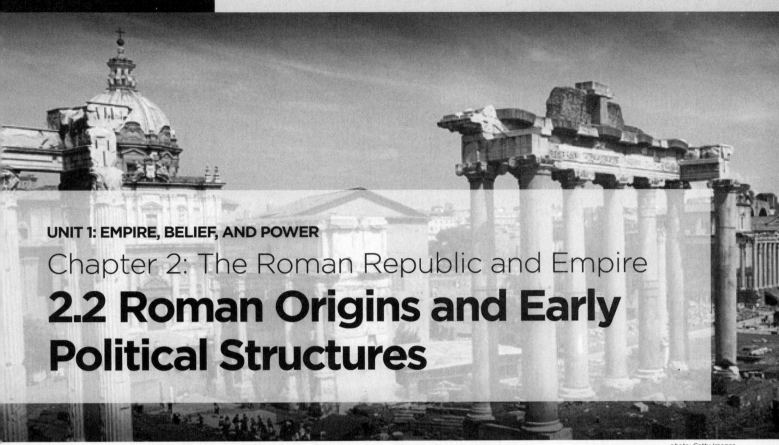

SOCIAL STUDIES
TECHBOOK

UNIT 1: EMPIRE, BELIEF, AND POWER

Chapter 2: The Roman Republic and Empire

2.2 Roman Origins and Early Political Structures

photo: Getty Images

LESSON OVERVIEW

Lesson Objectives:

By the end of this lesson, you should be able to:

- Trace the roots of Roman civilization to the contributions of Etruscans and Greek colonists.
- Analyze the political structure in ancient Rome and the democratic concepts developed in the region (separation of powers, representative government); compare to the democracies of Athens and of modern states.
- Describe the role of the Punic Wars in the growth of the Roman Empire.

Lesson Essential Question:

Was the Roman Republic democratic?

Key Vocabulary

Aeneas, Alps, assembly, bicameral, Carthage, census, Cincinnatus, citizen, code of law, Commodus, Constantine, consul, democracy, dictator, Diocletian, Emperor Augustus, Etruscans, Europe, Forum, Gaul, gladiator, Goths, Hannibal, Italy, Julius Caesar, jury, Latium, Mediterranean Sea, Octavian, oligarchy, Pantheon, patrician, peninsula, plebian, Punic Wars, Remus, representative, representative government, republic, Roman Empire, Roman Republic, Roman Senate, Rome, Romulus, Senate, Sicily, slavery, slaves, social class, Spain, Tiber River, tribune, Twelve Tables, Zama

FLASHCARDS

1 Rome's Early Influences

The early city of Rome was greatly influenced by the ancient Greek and Etruscan cultures.

- According to the Roman legends, Rome was founded by descendants of the Trojan hero Aeneas.
- Rome was ruled by Etruscan kings, who had overthrown the Latin kings.
- The Romans may have adopted the Etruscan alphabet, Etruscan and Greek gods, and Greek political philosophy.

Why Does It Matter?

The cultures that influenced Rome in its early history helped create Roman political philosophy and society, which have influenced many modern cultures.

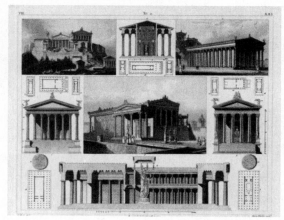

photo: Library of Congress

Greeks, Etruscans, and Latins all contributed to Roman ideas and culture.

2 The Roman Republic

The Roman Republic was a government in which the people elected their leaders. Roman citizens had certain rights and responsibilities.

- Patricians had most of the power at first, but over time plebeians fought for and won a significant role in their government.
- Rome's government was made up of three parts. Each had the ability to limit the power of the other parts.
- Romans created a written code of laws to ensure that people were treated fairly.

Why Does It Matter?

Many of the structures and principles of the Roman Republic influenced the creation of later democracies, including the United States.

photo: Library of Congress

The Romans created a republic and structured the government so that no one person or group could gain too much power.

FLASHCARDS *(continued)*

3 ▸ The Punic Wars

Between 264 and 146 BCE, Rome fought three wars, known as the Punic Wars, against the powerful city of Carthage.

- **In the first Punic War, Rome built up its army and gained the island of Sicily, as well as power in the Mediterranean Sea.**
- **In the second Punic War, the brilliant Carthaginian leader Hannibal almost captured Rome, but was eventually defeated by the Roman general Scipio.**
- **In the last Punic War, Rome defeated and destroyed Carthage.**

Why Does It Matter?

Through the Punic Wars, Rome gained power over the Mediterranean and a large amount of territory in North Africa and southern Europe. This expansion began the spread of the Roman Empire.

photo: From The New York Public Library

Between 264 BCE and 146 BCE, Rome fought three wars against Carthage and eventually gained control of all of the territory that had belonged to the North African power.

Name _____ **Date** _____

GRAPHIC ORGANIZER: Main Idea Web

Use this Main Idea Web to record information about early Roman history. For supporting resources, go to Empire, Belief, and Power > The Roman Republic and Empire > Roman Origins and Early Political Structures > Explore > The Roots of Roman Civilization.

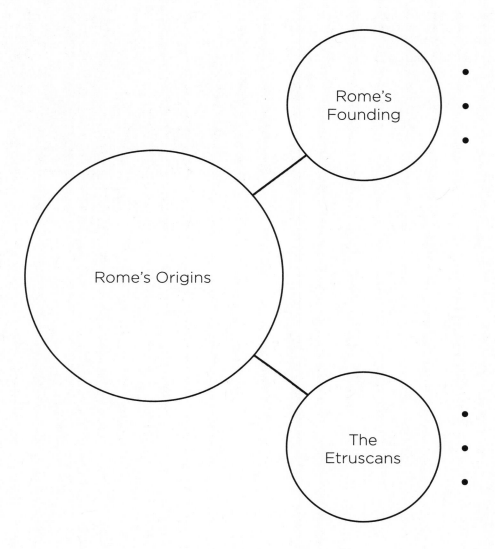

Rome's Founding

•

•

•

Rome's Origins

The Etruscans

•

•

•

Name _____ Date _____

GRAPHIC ORGANIZER: Cause/Event/Effect Chart

Use this Cause/Event/Effect Chart to record the causes that led to the creation of the Roman Republic and the effects the republic had on the people. For supporting resources, go to Empire, Belief, and Power > The Roman Republic and Empire > Roman Origins and Early Political Structures > Explore > The Roman Republic.

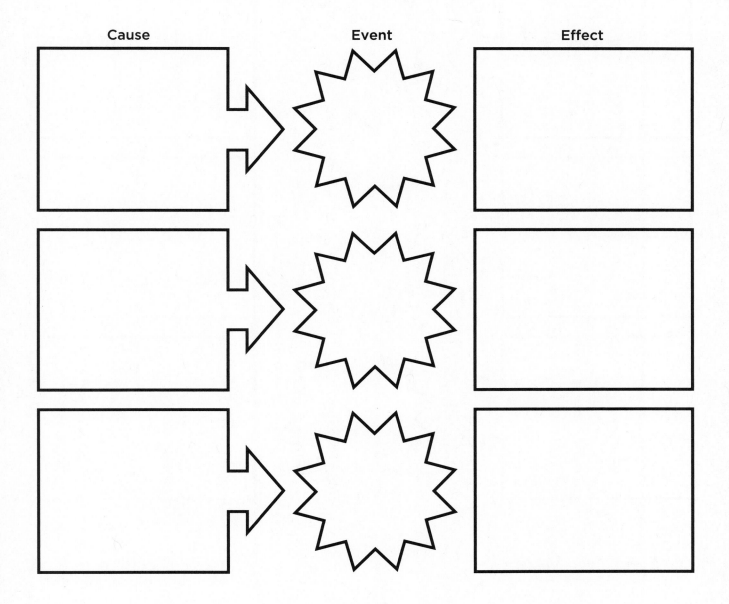

Cause · Event · Effect

Name _____ **Date** _____

GRAPHIC ORGANIZER: Cause/Event/Effect Chart *(continued)*

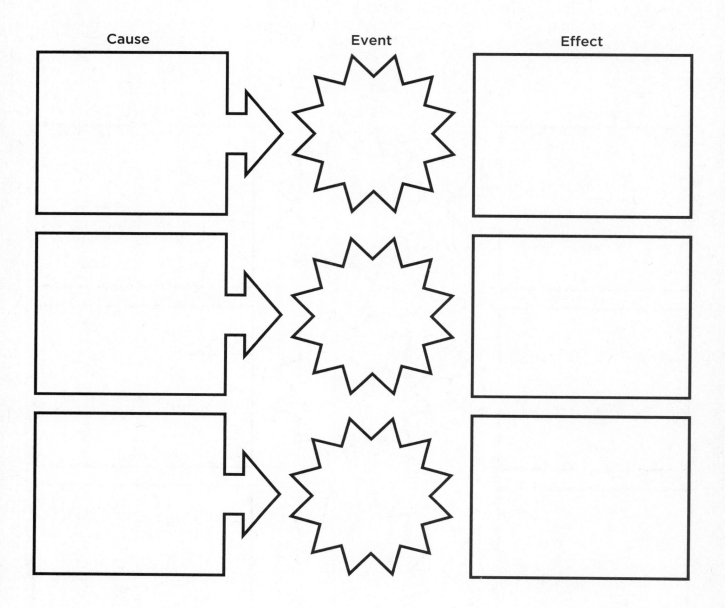

Cause   **Event**   **Effect**

Name _____ **Date** _____

GRAPHIC ORGANIZER: Main Idea Web

Use this Main Idea Web to record the democratic principles used in the government of ancient Rome. For supporting resources, go to Empire, Belief, and Power > The Roman Republic and Empire > Roman Origins and Early Political Structures > Explore > Principles of Democracy.

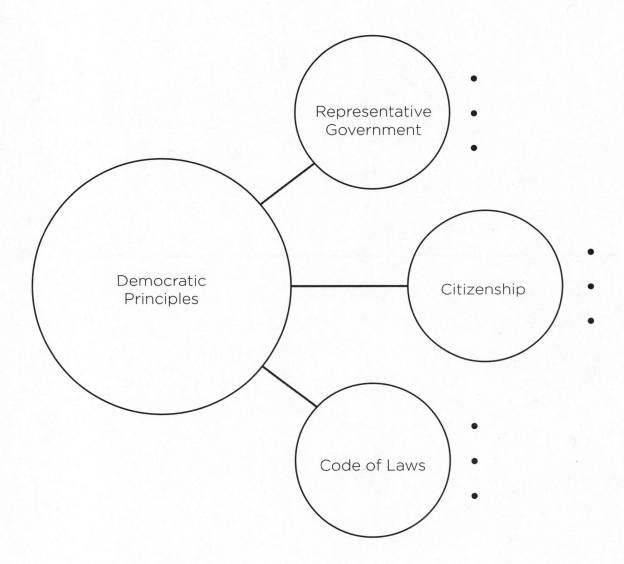

Name _____ **Date** _____

GRAPHIC ORGANIZER: Timeline

Complete this Timeline with the dates of each Punic war, the battle of Zama, and the territory gained. For supporting resources, go to Empire, Belief, and Power > The Roman Republic and Empire > Roman Origins and Early Political Structures > Explore > The Punic Wars.

264 BCE   146 BCE

◆━━━◆

Name _____ Date _____

EXPLORE: FOCUS QUESTIONS

Using what you learned from the Core Interactive Text, answer each page's focus question:

The Roots of Roman Civilization

How did the Roman civilization begin?

_____

_____

_____

The Etruscans

What role did the Etruscans play in Roman history?

_____

_____

_____

The Roman Republic

What form of government was established after the king was removed from power?

_____

_____

_____

Roman Government

What was Rome's political structure?

_____

_____

_____

Principles of Democracy

What democratic principles were present in the government of ancient Rome?

_____

_____

_____

The Punic Wars

What effect did the Punic Wars have on Rome?

_____

_____

_____

PROJECTS AND ASSESSMENTS

Explain Activities

ACTIVITY TYPE: DIAGRAM

Roman Origins and Early Political Structures

Use all the words from the Word Bank to create a graphic answer to the following question: How did different civilizations influence the development of early Roman culture? You may add any other words or symbols to complete your Mind Map. On a separate sheet of paper, summarize your ideas by responding to the statement at the bottom of the Mind Map. Be prepared to present your reasoning.

ACTIVITY TYPE: DIAGRAM

Roman Origins and Early Political Structures

The government of the ancient Roman Republic shares some similarities with the modern United States government. Use the Venn diagram to compare and contrast their characteristics.

ACTIVITY TYPE: SOCIAL STUDIES EXPLANATION

Roman Origins and Early Political Structures

In this Social Studies Explanation activity, you will use a template to assemble evidence from the sources you have explored. Then, you will write an answer to the Essential Question and defend your answer with supporting evidence.

Elaborate Activities

photo:Discovery Education

INVESTIGATION TYPE: HISTORICAL PERSPECTIVES

Roman Society

Your mission is to get to know four individuals from ancient Roman society at the time of the Republic and explore the perspectives you think each would have on key issues of the day.

PROJECTS AND ASSESSMENTS *(continued)*

photo: Library of Congress

ACTIVITY TYPE: CURRENT EVENTS CONNECTION

Ancient Roots of Modern Government

In this activity, you will give a presentation for Constitution Day, a day that celebrates the adoption of the U.S. Constitution. In your presentation, you will discuss the influence of Greek and Roman governments on the U.S. government today.

photo: Library of Congress

ACTIVITY TYPE: ROLE PLAY

Roman Origins and Early Political Structures

In this activity, you will take on the role of either a patrician or a plebeian and write a journal entry describing how you feel about the plebeian struggle for power and equality.

photo: Getty Images

ACTIVITY TYPE: DOCUMENT-BASED INVESTIGATION

Democratic Ideals of Ancient Rome

In this activity, you will write a newspaper article and a speech addressing the people of Rome. In what ways was the civilization of ancient Rome democratic? In what ways was it not democratic?

Evaluate Activities

BRIEF-CONSTRUCTED RESPONSE (BCR)

Roman Origins and Early Political Structures

EXTENDED-CONSTRUCTED RESPONSE (ECR)

Roman Origins and Early Political Structures

UNIT 1: EMPIRE, BELIEF, AND POWER

Chapter 2: The Roman Republic and Empire

2.3 From Republic to Empire

photo: Getty Images

LESSON OVERVIEW

Lesson Objectives:

By the end of this lesson, you should be able to:

- **Analyze the causes and effects of Rome's transition from a Republic to an Empire.**
- **Trace the expansion of the Roman Empire from the rise of Caesar to 476 CE.**

Lesson Essential Question:

How did Rome's transition from Republic to Empire impact its citizens?

Key Vocabulary

aqueduct, Brutus, Caligula, Carthage, Charlemagne, citizen, Claudius, Cleopatra VII, consul, dictator, Egypt, Emperor Augustus, Greece, Hannibal, Julius Caesar, Macedonia, Mark Antony, Mediterranean Sea, Middle East, Nero, Octavian, Pax Romana, Ptolemy, Roman Empire, Roman Republic, Rome, Rubicon River, Spain, Tiberius, triumvirate

SOCIAL STUDIES TECHBOOK

FLASHCARDS

1 Rome Becomes an Empire

Julius Caesar's defeat of Pompey led to the end of the Roman Republic and the founding of the Roman Empire.

- Caesar was originally Pompey's ally in the First Triumvirate.
- Caesar's victory in Gaul gave him the political strength to defeat Pompey.
- Some members of the Roman Senate were worried about Caesar's growing power and had him assassinated.
- Octavian, Caesar's nephew, won the civil war that followed Caesar's death and became Augustus, the emperor.

Why Does It Matter?

Rome's transformation from a Republic to an Empire meant that the citizens no longer had a say in who ruled them. Instead, the title of emperor was passed down through family lines.

photo: Pixabay

This is a Roman statue of Julius Caesar, who founded the Roman Empire.

2 The Growth of the Empire

The Roman Empire expanded quickly in its first 100 years. Eventually the Empire grew too large to be governed easily.

- Rome's location on the Mediterranean Sea and the warm climate of that location made it easy to expand.
- Conquered nations were absorbed into the Empire. Cities were built to resemble Rome, and the Roman culture was passed on to the new citizens.
- While the Empire itself was run in an orderly fashion, the transfer of the role of emperor involved a great deal of violence and intrigue.

Why Does It Matter?

The Pax Romana brought an end to the internal fighting that had plagued Rome since the time of Caesar. During this period, Rome's expansion brought great wealth and cultural diversity to the Empire and the people living in it. Many people were happy to become a part of Rome because of the many advantages the Romans brought, including better architecture, education, and health. A common language, calendar, religion, and currency helped tie the Empire together.

photo: Getty's Open Content Program

Most of the empire's expansion took place under Augustus and Hadrian.

Name _____ **Date** _____

GRAPHIC ORGANIZER: Sequencing Chart

Use this Sequencing Chart to record events in the rise of the Roman Empire. For supporting resources, go to Empire, Belief, and Power > The Roman Republic and Empire > From Republic to Empire > Explore > The Rise of Julius Caesar.

Event	Date	Summary

Name _____ **Date** _____

GRAPHIC ORGANIZER: Sequencing Chart *(continued)*

Event	Date	Summary

Name _____ **Date** _____

GRAPHIC ORGANIZER: Main Idea Web

Use this Main Idea Web to take notes on the Roman Empire. For supporting resources, go to Empire, Belief, and Power > The Roman Republic and Empire > From Republic to Empire > Explore > Portrait of an Empire.

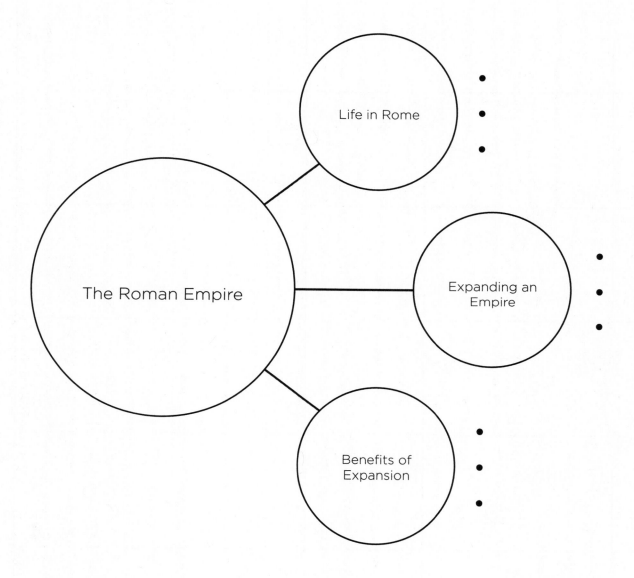

Name _____ Date _____

EXPLORE: FOCUS QUESTIONS

Using what you learned from the Core Interactive Text, answer each page's focus question:

The Rise of Julius Caesar

How did Julius Caesar come to power?

_____

_____

_____

Dictator for Life

How did Julius Caesar become dictator for life?

_____

_____

_____

The Ides of March

Why was Julius Caesar murdered?

_____

_____

_____

Civil War

How was stability restored to Rome after the death of Julius Caesar?

_____

_____

_____

The Dynastic Tradition

How was power transferred in the Roman Empire?

_____

_____

_____

Name _____ **Date** _____

EXPLORE: FOCUS QUESTIONS *(continued)*

Portrait of an Empire
What was life like in the Roman Empire?

_____
_____
_____
_____

The Empire Grows
How did the Roman Empire expand?

_____
_____
_____
_____

The Benefits of Expansion
How did expansion benefit the Roman Empire?

_____
_____
_____
_____

PROJECTS AND ASSESSMENTS

Explain Activities

ACTIVITY TYPE: MOVIE TRAILER

From Republic to Empire

In this activity, you will use story frames to create a scene from a movie trailer for a new film about the rise and expansion of the Roman Empire.

ACTIVITY TYPE: YOU AS JOURNALIST

From Republic to Empire

In this activity, you will write an informational piece to investigate an event that led to changes in Rome's political system from a republic to an empire, including the cause of the event and the result, or effect, of the event.

ACTIVITY TYPE: SOCIAL STUDIES EXPLANATION

From Republic to Empire

In this Social Studies Explanation activity, you will use a template to assemble evidence from the sources you have explored. Then, you will write an answer to the Essential Question and defend your answer with supporting evidence.

Elaborate Activities

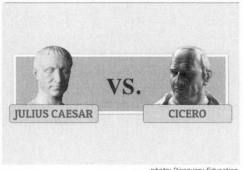

photo: Discovery Education

INVESTIGATION TYPE: ENDURING DEBATE

Julius Caesar vs. Cicero

Is the traditional republican form of government the best way to rule the Roman Empire?

photo: Getty Images

ACTIVITY TYPE: ROLE PLAY

From Republic to Empire

In this activity, you will take on the role of either Octavian or Mark Antony and participate in a mediation session during which you will try to resolve your differences and come to terms with a fellow student playing the part of your rival.

PROJECTS AND ASSESSMENTS *(continued)*

photo: Pixabay

ACTIVITY TYPE: CLASSROOM DEBATE

From Republic to Empire

In this activity, you will learn about the early Roman Empire and determine how the shift from the republican era affected life for ordinary Romans. After you have completed your research, you will participate in a debate.

photo: Getty Images

ACTIVITY TYPE: DOCUMENT-BASED INVESTIGATION

The Real Julius Caesar

In this Document-Based Investigation, you will analyze and synthesize information from a variety of primary and secondary source documents to develop and defend an argument about Julius Caesar's rule over Rome.

Evaluate Activities

BRIEF-CONSTRUCTED RESPONSE (BCR)

From Republic to Empire

EXTENDED-CONSTRUCTED RESPONSE (ECR)

From Republic to Empire

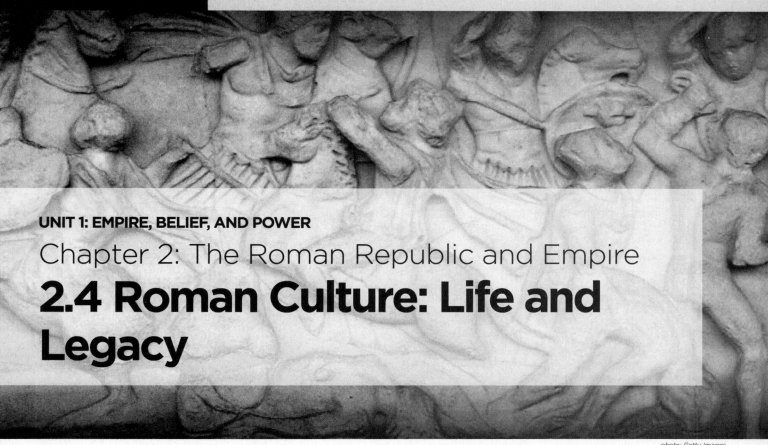

UNIT 1: EMPIRE, BELIEF, AND POWER

Chapter 2: The Roman Republic and Empire

2.4 Roman Culture: Life and Legacy

photo: Getty Images

LESSON OVERVIEW

Lesson Objectives:

By the end of this lesson, you should be able to:

- **Analyze relationships of power between Roman rulers, citizens, and slaves.**
- **Analyze the impact of Roman government infrastructure programs on Roman life and culture and on life and culture today.**
- **Trace the influence of the Roman Empire on language.**

Key Vocabulary

aqueduct, architecture, census, Circus Maximus, Colosseum, Egypt, Emperor Augustus, Europe, gladiator, hierarchy, irrigation, Latin, legionnaires, North Africa, Octavian, Pantheon, paterfamilias, patrician, Pax Romana, Phoenicians, plebian, Roman Empire, Rome, Sicily, taxes, Twelve Tables

Lesson Essential Question:

How did the spread of Roman culture influence life throughout the Empire?

FLASHCARDS

1 ## Power Relationships in Rome Before the Empire

Roman society was dominated by men and was very hierarchical, traditional, and family-oriented. The structure of Roman society was mirrored by the structure of the Roman family.

- During the early republic:
  - In the family, the power resided in the hands of the paterfamilias (father of the family); below him were subordinate men, then the women and enslaved persons.
  - In a patrician family, there might also be clients, who were plebeians who had pledged loyalty.
  - A small group of rich men of the patrician class formed the governing body, the Senate.
  - Plebeians were more numerous than patricians but could not participate in government.
  - Plebeians fought to gain increased political power and to establish the Twelve Tables, the basic law code of ancient Rome.
- After the establishment of the empire:
  - Society was still dominated by men, but women had more of a life outside the home.
  - Power shifted into the hands of the emperors.
  - The number of enslaved people increased until they greatly outnumbered the plebeians, putting the plebeians out of work.
  - Emperors employed "bread and circuses" to keep unemployed plebeians from rioting.
  - Slavery supported the empire. Enslaved people could buy their freedom on occasion.
  - Slave revolts rocked the empire and instilled a long-lasting fear of slavery in the ruling class.

Why Does It Matter?

The ideas in the Twelve Tables provided the principles of law adopted by the republic and inspired the creators of the French and American democracies. Also, the more Rome exerted its power over the rest of the known world through conquest, the more Roman citizens gave up their own power, until Rome's republic became an empire. Rome never stopped being a hierarchical society with power in the hands of the wealthy few. This division between the classes would lead to later problems.

photo: Library of Congress

The social hierarchy in Rome led to a wide gap between the rich and poor.

FLASHCARDS *(continued)*

2 ▸ Roman Genius

By developing roads, aqueducts, a common currency, a code of law, and introducing practical reforms, Rome created order over an immense area with an extraordinary diversity of people and languages, which allowed the spread of its cultural achievements.

- Roman engineers and architects develop techniques and styles that are uniquely their own.
- Communal baths spread throughout the empire.
- Invention of concrete explains in part why so many Roman buildings and roads throughout the empire still survive.
- Rome uses Greek building styles but also added its own architectural strategies (vaults, arches, use of concrete) to build larger, taller, and heavier buildings.
- Greco-Roman art strongly influences Renaissance artists.

Why Does It Matter?

Rome's cultural achievements would not have had such a broad impact if Rome had not had a well-developed infrastructure, bureaucracy, and administration. The infrastructure created order. Because of this organization, some cultures actually welcomed conquest because it brought order. In general, Rome did not enslave the conquered peoples; they became citizens and thus could be taxed. Roman cultural achievements were able to spread far and wide because of these conquests. Many of the achievements of Rome still impact our lives today.

photo: Library of Congress

The technological achievements of ancient Rome, such as roads and aqueducts, helped its leaders maintain control over the expanding empire.

3 ▸ The Development of Language

Latin is a practical language for a practical people. Its ability to absorb the innovations of other cultures and still retain its own identity underlines its continued existence in scientific and legal terminology. Although people do not speak it today, it has had a significant impact on the descendants of the Roman Empire.

- Latin became the common language of the Roman Empire.
- Latin became the official language of the Roman Catholic Church.
- Latin is still used in terminology for law, science, and mathematics. The spread of Latin transformed the languages of European tribes, resulting in the formation of various Romance languages.
- English contains many Latin-based words.
- The Latin alphabet and script became more widespread than any other and became the basis for the modern English alphabet.

Why Does It Matter?

Latin's remarkable resilience and transformation into the common language of the Mediterranean region brought people who spoke different languages closer; it enabled them to communicate across the divides of culture, class, and history.

photo: Library of Congress

The Gutenberg Bible, the first book printed in the Western world, was printed in Latin.

Name _____ **Date** _____

GRAPHIC ORGANIZER: GREASES Chart

Use this GREASES Chart to record characteristics of Roman culture. For supporting resources, go to Empire, Belief, and Power > The Roman Republic and Empire > Roman Culture: Life and Legacy > Explore > Roman Society.

Government	
Religion	
Economic	
Art & Architecture	
Science & Technology	
Environment	
Social & Cultural Values	

Name _____ **Date** _____

GRAPHIC ORGANIZER: Comparison Chart

Use this Comparison Chart to compare and contrast the roles and responsibilities of citizens from various social classes in Rome. For supporting resources, go to Empire, Belief, and Power > The Roman Republic and Empire > Roman Culture: Life and Legacy > Explore > Patrons and Clients.

Criteria	Roles	Responsibilities
Patricians		
Plebians		
Women		
Slaves		

Name _____ Date _____

EXPLORE: FOCUS QUESTIONS

Using what you learned from the Core Interactive Text, answer each page's focus question:

Roman Society

How was Roman society structured?

_____
_____
_____

Patrons and Clients

What was patronage?

_____
_____
_____

Slavery in Ancient Rome

What role did slavery play in the Roman Empire?

_____
_____
_____

Bread and Circuses

How did the ruling classes attempt to keep the poorer members of society happy?

_____
_____
_____

Pax Romana

What led to the Pax Romana?

_____
_____
_____

Name _____ Date _____

EXPLORE: FOCUS QUESTIONS *(continued)*

Moving People, Moving Water
How did public projects impact culture in the Roman Empire?

_____

_____

_____

A Practical Art
What kind of influence has Roman art and architecture had on Western culture?

_____

_____

_____

Latin: Dead or Alive
How did Latin influence the world?

_____

_____

_____

PROJECTS AND ASSESSMENTS

Explain Activities

ACTIVITY TYPE: DIAGRAM

Roman Culture: Life and Legacy

In this activity, you will use a mind map to create a graphic explanation of the structure of power in ancient Roman society, which includes the structure of family power.

ACTIVITY TYPE: YOU AS JOURNALIST

Roman Culture: Life and Legacy

In this activity, you will imagine you live in the city of Smyrna after it has been conquered by Rome.

ACTIVITY TYPE: SOCIAL STUDIES EXPLANATION

Roman Culture: Life and Legacy

In this Social Studies Explanation activity, you will use a template to assemble evidence from the sources you have explored. Then, you will write an answer to the Essential Question and defend your answer with supporting evidence.

Elaborate Activities

photo: Getty Images

INVESTIGATION TYPE: MAP-GUIDED INQUIRY

All Roads Lead to Rome

How did Roman culture spread throughout the provinces of the Roman Empire? What evidence of Roman occupation can still be found today? In this investigation, you will use the Map-Guided Inquiry interactive tool to examine how ancient Roman culture influenced the world around it and continues to affect us today.

photo: Getty Images

ACTIVITY TYPE: PITCH YOUR IDEA

Bid for Bridge Construction

In this activity, you will create a slideshow presentation to deliver before the Roman governor of Spain describing your construction plan and explaining why your company should be the one awarded the project.

PROJECTS AND ASSESSMENTS *(continued)*

photo: Getty's Open Content Program

ACTIVITY TYPE: SAY WHAT?

"Bread and Circuses"

In this activity, you will translate an excerpt from ancient Roman text into modern language, draw or diagram its main idea, and analyze its relevance to the society and culture of ancient Rome.

photo: Getty Images

ACTIVITY TYPE: DOCUMENT-BASED INVESTIGATION

Class Structure in Roman Society

In this activity, you will analyze the roles of the various classes in ancient Roman society and the power that each class had. You will also trace how the classes were affected and changed by developments in Roman culture over time.

Evaluate Activities

BRIEF-CONSTRUCTED RESPONSE (BCR)

Roman Culture: Life and Legacy

EXTENDED-CONSTRUCTED RESPONSE (ECR)

Roman Culture: Life and Legacy

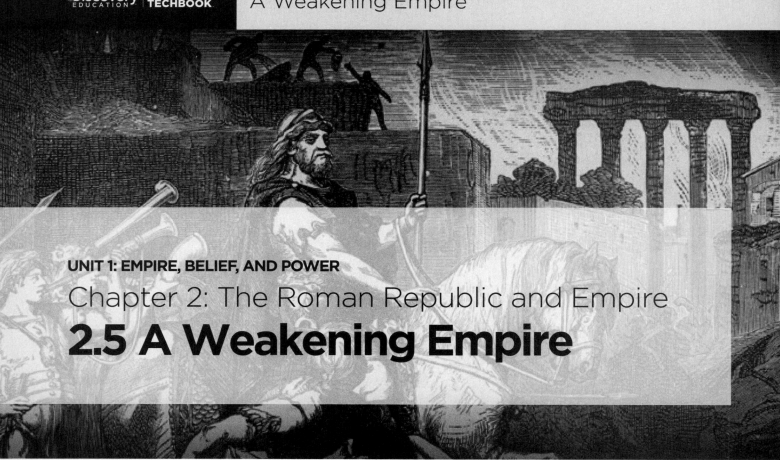

UNIT 1: EMPIRE, BELIEF, AND POWER

Chapter 2: The Roman Republic and Empire

2.5 A Weakening Empire

LESSON OVERVIEW

Lesson Objectives:

By the end of this lesson, you should be able to:

- Analyze and explain the political, geographic, and cultural factors that led to the fall of the Roman Empire.

- Explain how Constantine's establishment of the new capital in Constantinople helped lead to the Western Empire's fall.

- Describe the sack of Rome and analyze the impact of the dismantling of the empire.

Lesson Essential Question:

Why did Rome decline and fall?

Key Vocabulary

Alaric, Attila, Battle of Adrianople, Byzantine Empire, Catholicism / Roman Catholicism, Celtic peoples, Christianity, citizen, Constantine, Constantinople, Diocletian, Division of the Roman Empire, Eastern Orthodox Christianity, empire, Gaul, Germanic peoples, Goths, Huns, migration, nomadic, province, Roman Empire, Roman Senate, Rome, Spain, taxes, technology, trade

FLASHCARDS

1 Decline

After the year 180, political, geographic, and cultural factors led the Roman Empire into gradual weakness and eventual collapse.

- For nearly a century, Rome had no orderly transfer of power as emperors replaced one another by force, bribery, and murder.
- Leaders gave no thought to the general welfare of the state but sought power only to enrich themselves.
- High taxes to pay for the army and for bribes to enemy leaders drove Romans into poverty and crippled trade.
- Migration of the Huns, a nomadic people of Asia, frightened the Germanic tribes and drove them toward Roman territory.

Why Does It Matter?

Rome was the most powerful state the world had known to that time, but its power was undermined by forces inside and outside the empire.

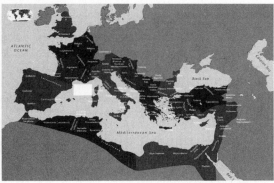

photo: Discovery Education

The constant warfare of the 200s crippled the economy of the Roman Empire.

2 Diocletian and Constantine

After Diocletian restored order and organization, Constantine radically changed the structure of the empire.

- Diocletian restored order to the empire and reorganized the government.
- Diocletian gave up his throne, and his new government fell.
- Constantine won the struggle for power that followed Diocletian's rule and appointed himself emperor.
- Constantine saw that the city of Rome itself was no longer important to the life of the empire.
- Constantine moved the capital of the empire from Rome to a new city, which he named for himself.
- The Western Roman Empire was heavily taxed to pay for defense of the east and was left without adequate defenses against the Germanic tribes.

Why Does It Matter?

The Eastern Roman Empire remained intact during the barbarian invasions, while the Western Empire collapsed.

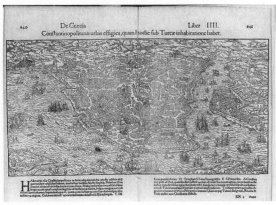

photo: Library of Congress

How did Constantine's decision to found a new capital lead to the decline of the city of Rome and of Rome itself?

FLASHCARDS *(continued)*

3 ▶ Fall

The city of Rome was sacked several times by Germanic tribes, and the empire broke apart.

- Alaric the Goth was the first Germanic king to sack Rome, in 410.
- The invasion of the empire by the Huns, under their leader Attila, eventually caused the Germanic tribes to break up the empire.
- Odoacer, another Gothic chieftain, deposed the last Roman emperor in the west in 476.
- After the fall of the Western Roman Empire, Europe was broken into separate kingdoms, most ruled by Germanic tribes.
- Roman cultural traditions were lost as Western Europe sank into its "Dark Ages."
- The Eastern Roman Empire survived as the Byzantine Empire until 1453.

Why Does It Matter?

The destruction of a strong political and cultural tradition led to centuries of disorder and hardship until new traditions evolved.

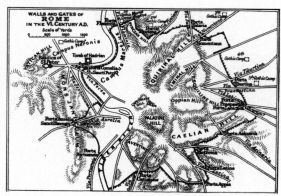

photo: Procopius. History of the Wars. Vol. 3. Trans. H. B. Dewing. New York, NY: G. P. Putnam's Sons, 1919.

Despite many walls and gates, the Roman Empire was invaded several times.

Name _____ **Date** _____

GRAPHIC ORGANIZER: GREASES Chart

Use this GREASES Chart to record information about Roman society in the period before and during the empire's decline and fall. For supporting resources, go to Empire, Belief, and Power > The Roman Republic and Empire > A Weakening Empire > Explore > Who Was Emperor? Who Was Not Emperor?

Government	
Religion	
Economic	
Art & Architecture	
Science & Technology	
Environment	
Social & Cultural Values	

Discovery SOCIAL STUDIES
EDUCATION TECHBOOK

Name _____ Date _____

GRAPHIC ORGANIZER: Cause/Event/Effect Chart

Use this Cause/Event/Effect Chart to list the causes and effects of each event related to the decline and fall of the Roman Empire. For supporting resources, go to Empire, Belief, and Power > The Roman Republic and Empire > A Weakening Empire > Explore > Attacks from the East.

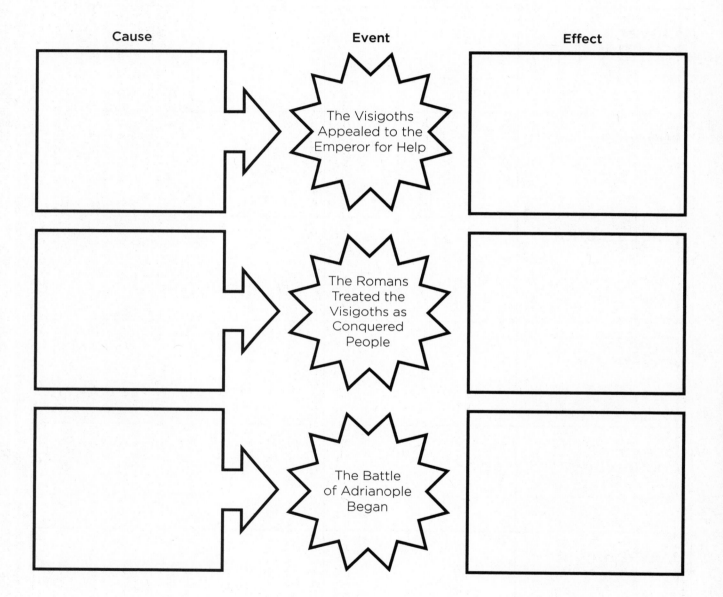

Cause   Event   Effect

The Visigoths Appealed to the Emperor for Help

The Romans Treated the Visigoths as Conquered People

The Battle of Adrianople Began

Discovery EDUCATION | SOCIAL STUDIES TECHBOOK

Name _____ **Date** _____

GRAPHIC ORGANIZER: Cause/Event/Effect Chart *(continued)*

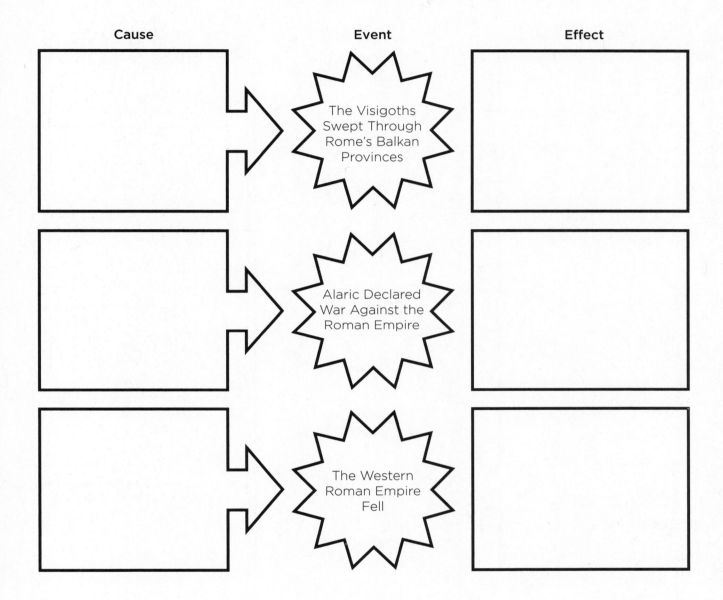

Cause   Event   Effect

The Visigoths Swept Through Rome's Balkan Provinces

Alaric Declared War Against the Roman Empire

The Western Roman Empire Fell

Name _____ Date _____

GRAPHIC ORGANIZER: Cause/Event/Effect Chart *(continued)*

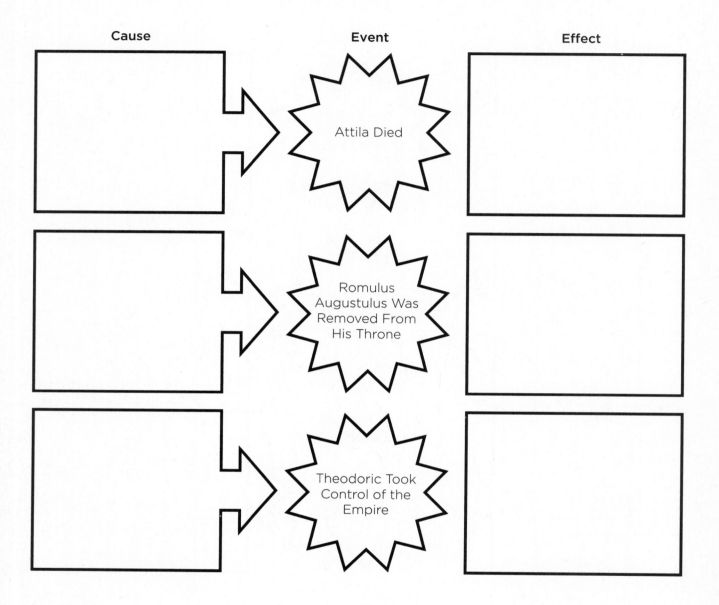

Cause	Event	Effect
	Attila Died	
	Romulus Augustulus Was Removed From His Throne	
	Theodoric Took Control of the Empire	

Name _____ Date _____

EXPLORE: FOCUS QUESTIONS

Using what you learned from the Core Interactive Text, answer each page's focus question:

Who Was Emperor? Who Was Not Emperor?
How did Rome become politically unstable?

_____

_____

_____

Chaos in the Armies
How did internal conflict weaken the empire?

_____

_____

_____

Beyond the Frontier
Who were the barbarian tribes?

_____

_____

_____

The Empire Divided
Why was the capital of the Roman Empire moved?

_____

_____

_____

The Empire in the East
How did Constantinople become Rome's second capital?

_____

_____

_____

Name _____ Date _____

EXPLORE: FOCUS QUESTIONS *(continued)*

Attacks from the East
Why did Germanic tribes attack Rome?

_____
_____
_____

The Fall of Rome
How did Rome fall to Germanic tribes?

_____
_____
_____

After the Fall of Rome
What happened after the fall of the Western Roman Empire?

_____
_____
_____

Discovery | SOCIAL STUDIES
EDUCATION | **TECHBOOK**

PROJECTS AND ASSESSMENTS

Explain Activities

ACTIVITY TYPE: VISUALIZATION

A Weakening Empire

Choose the most important events or trends that contributed to the decline and fall of the Roman Empire. Diagram the events or trends in order of their importance, from the sixth-most important to the most important overall. Add a title, illustrate the events or trends, and justify your ranking below each illustration with a caption.

ACTIVITY TYPE: YOU AS JOURNALIST

A Weakening Empire

In this activity, you will interview an eyewitness to the events leading to the decline and fall of the Roman Empire.

ACTIVITY TYPE: SOCIAL STUDIES EXPLANATION

A Weakening Empire

In this Social Studies Explanation activity, you will use a template to assemble evidence from the sources you have explored. Then, you will write an answer to the Essential Question and defend your answer with supporting evidence.

Elaborate Activities

INVESTIGATION TYPE: TIMELINE MAP

The Harder They Fall

Was Rome destroyed by outside enemies or by weakness within the empire itself? Your mission is to explore the events leading up to the fall of the Western Roman Empire, from 180 to 476, and identify the main reasons for Rome's fall.

photo: Getty Images

PROJECTS AND ASSESSMENTS *(continued)*

photo: Library of Congress

ACTIVITY TYPE: CLASSROOM SPEECH

Addressing the Roman Senate

In this activity, you will prepare a speech for delivery to the Senate on how the actions of the armies are weakening the empire and what you believe should be done about it.

photo: Library of Congress

ACTIVITY TYPE: PITCH YOUR IDEA

Learning from the Past

In this activity, you will use the example of Rome and at least one other ancient empire to create and deliver a proposal to a modern ruler.

photo: Getty Images

ACTIVITY TYPE: DOCUMENT-BASED INVESTIGATION

A Weakening Empire

In this Document-Based Investigation, you will analyze source materials and investigate this question: In a recent scholarly article, Professor Know-It-All claimed that during his reign, "Emperor Constantine I did more harm than good to the declining Roman Empire." Did he or didn't he?

Evaluate Activities

BRIEF-CONSTRUCTED RESPONSE (BCR)

A Weakening Empire

EXTENDED-CONSTRUCTED RESPONSE (ECR)

A Weakening Empire

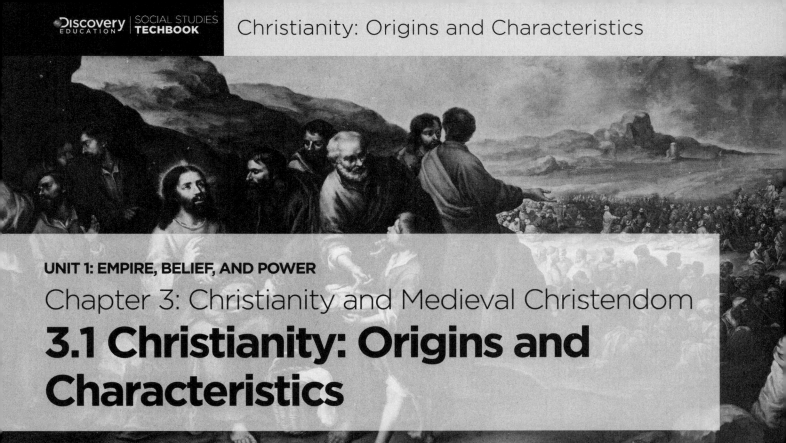

UNIT 1: EMPIRE, BELIEF, AND POWER

Chapter 3: Christianity and Medieval Christendom
3.1 Christianity: Origins and Characteristics

photo: Getty's Open Content Program

LESSON OVERVIEW

Lesson Objectives:

By the end of this lesson, you should be able to:

- **Explain the origins of Christianity based on the life and teachings of Jesus.**
- **Describe the characteristics of Christianity.**

Lesson Essential Question:

How did Christianity develop?

Key Vocabulary

Abraham, apostle, beginning of Christianity, Bethlehem, bishop, Christianity, Constantine, Hebrews, Herod the Great, Israel, Jerusalem, Jesus, Judaism, Judea, King David, King Solomon, Mecca, Messiah, missionary, monotheism, Moses, Muhammad, Nazareth, Nebuchadnezzar, New Testament, Palestine, parable, Phoenicians, polytheism, proselytizing religion / universalizing religion, Roman Empire, Rome, Ruth, Saul, Ten Commandments

FLASHCARDS

1 The Life and Teachings of Jesus

Christians believe that Jesus Christ lived and taught in Israel at the start of the Common Era.

- Israel was under the control of the Roman Empire.
- The life and teachings of Jesus are written in the Gospels of the four apostles: Matthew, Mark, Luke, and John.
- Love of God and compassion for other people are the primary rules of Christianity.
- Christians believe that Jesus died and was resurrected.
- Christianity was outlawed by the Roman Empire until Emperor Constantine made it the official religion in the 200s.

Why Does It Matter?

The origins of Christianity in Roman-controlled Judea and the story behind the life and teachings of Jesus are crucial to understanding how Christianity became such a widespread religion.

photo: Library of Congress

This painting is an artist's depiction of Jesus's resurrection.

2 Characteristics of Christianity

Christianity is the belief that Jesus Christ was the human son of God and that he died to redeem the sins of humanity.

- The Christian Bible includes both the Old Testament and the New Testament.
- Christians believe in the same God as the Jews. They follow some Jewish laws, like the Ten Commandments, but not others.
- Many Christians proselytize, or actively try to convert people to Christianity.

Why Does It Matter?

Christianity developed out of Judaism and kept some of its laws and customs. The Christian practice of proselytizing has helped make it one of the largest and most diverse religions in the world.

photo: Pixabay

The Old Testament of the Christian Bible contains many of the same biblical books as the Jewish Torah. The New Testament is exclusive to the Christian Bible.

Name _____ **Date** _____

GRAPHIC ORGANIZER: Sequencing Chart

Use this Sequencing Chart to create a timeline of the life of Jesus. For supporting resources, go to Empire, Belief, and Power > Christianity and Medieval Christendom > Christianity: Origins and Characteristics > Explore > The Birth of Jesus.

Event	Importance to Religion

Name _____ Date _____

EXPLORE: FOCUS QUESTIONS

Using what you learned from the Core Interactive Text, answer each page's focus question:

Judea Under Roman Rule
What was Judea like when Christianity began to develop?

_____
_____
_____

The Birth of Jesus
What do Christians believe about the birth of Jesus?

_____
_____
_____

Who Was Jesus?
What do Christians believe about Jesus's life?

_____
_____
_____

Jesus's Teachings
What were the teachings of Jesus?

_____
_____
_____

Building the Bible
What was included in the Christian Bible?

_____
_____
_____

Spreading the Faith
How did Christianity spread?

_____
_____
_____

PROJECTS AND ASSESSMENTS

Explain Activities

ACTIVITY TYPE: DIAGRAM

Christianity: Origins and Characteristics

In this activity, you will use a 3-Way Venn Diagram to compare the major beliefs of two ancient religions, or belief systems, with Christianity.

ACTIVITY TYPE: DIAGRAM

Christianity: Origins and Characteristics

In this activity, you will use at least 10 words from the word bank to create a mind map graphic response to the Essential Question.

ACTIVITY TYPE: SOCIAL STUDIES EXPLANATION

Christianity: Origins and Characteristics

In this Social Studies Explanation activity, you will use a template to assemble evidence from the sources you have explored. Then, you will write an answer to the Essential Question and defend your answer with supporting evidence.

Elaborate Activities

photo: Getty Images

INVESTIGATION TYPE: SOURCE ANALYSIS

Tenets of Christianity

How did stained glass windows in medieval churches help teach the basic tenets of Christianity through allegorical scenes from the Bible or Gospels? In this investigation, you will analyze a stained glass window and find evidence of how these works of art were used to advance the Christian faith.

photo: Library of Congress

ACTIVITY TYPE: SAY WHAT?

The Sermon on the Mount

In this activity, you will translate excerpts from the Sermon on the Mount into modern language.

PROJECTS AND ASSESSMENTS *(continued)*

photo: Getty's Open Content Program

ACTIVITY TYPE: DOCUMENT-BASED INVESTIGATION

Christianity: Origins and Characteristics

In this Document-Based Investigation, you will be analyzing the interactions between early Christians and the Romans. As you analyze the sources, investigate this question: Why did Roman officials persecute Christians?

Evaluate Activities

BRIEF-CONSTRUCTED RESPONSE (BCR)

Christianity: Origins and Characteristics

EXTENDED-CONSTRUCTED RESPONSE (ECR)

Christianity: Origins and Characteristics

photo: Getty Images

LESSON OVERVIEW

Lesson Objectives:

By the end of this lesson, you should be able to:

- Analyze the factors that led to the diffusion of Christianity throughout the Roman Empire and other parts of Europe.
- Explain the importance of monks, missionaries, and the Christian church itself in the spread of Christianity throughout Europe.
- Describe the impact of the fall of the Western Roman Empire on Christianity.

Key Vocabulary

bishop, Catholic Church, Christianity, Constantine, convert, disciple, missionary, monastery, monk, Paul, pope, propaganda, proselytizing religion / universalizing religion, Saint Anthony, Saint Patrick

Lesson Essential Question:

How did Christianity become the world's largest religion?

FLASHCARDS

1 The Diffusion of Christianity

Christianity spread throughout the Roman Empire and other parts of Europe for a number of reasons and with a variety of results.

- After Jesus's death, his disciples spread his word and convinced others to become Christians.
- Because Christians put God before the emperor, they were persecuted by Roman officials.
- Christianity's message of equality, hope, and salvation made it appealing to many, especially those in the lower classes.
- As Rome's culture spread, so did Christianity.
- Roman Emperor Constantine adopted Christianity in 312, ending the persecution of Christians.

Why Does It Matter?

Christianity overcame many obstacles to become a popular religion. Early worshipers suffered persecution and harassment for their beliefs until Christianity became widespread. Today, early adopters of radical ideas often endure public scrutiny and criticism until their ideas become accepted.

photo: IRC

Steles like this commemorated important events in Roman life. This one shows a Christian being immersed in water to be baptized.

2 Key Players in the Spread of Christianity

Monks, missionaries, and the Christian church itself were important in the spread of Christianity throughout Europe.

- Missionaries traveled to areas where people were not Christian and convinced them to join their faith.
- Monasteries were communities for monks who dedicated their lives to prayer and service to God.
- Christianity spread from Jerusalem into Syria, Egypt, and elsewhere, until most Roman citizens were Christian.

Why Does It Matter?

The Christian religion spread rapidly. Some believers moved around to find new converts, and some servants of the church stayed in their communities to serve worshipers there. Missionaries are still active around the world, working to convert others to Christianity.

photo: Library of Congress

This is a figure of a monk.

FLASHCARDS *(continued)*

3 The Church Splits

By 1054, Christianity had spread across Europe, parts of Asia, and parts of Africa. But disagreements over how Christianity should be practiced splintered the church.

- **Church leaders in the East and West disagreed over how much power the pope should have.**
- **In 1054, the Christian church split.**
- **The Orthodox Church rose in the East.**
- **The Catholic Church rose in the West..**

Why Does It Matter?

Disagreements over church practices still exist in the Christian church. The church has several different denominations, or subgroups, that view and practice Christianity in different ways.

photo: Pixabay

After the schism, the Eastern Orthodox church developed its own traditions and thrived.

Name _____ **Date** _____

GRAPHIC ORGANIZER: Comparison Chart

Use this Cause/Event/Effect Chart to explore the different factors that affected the spread of Christianity. For supporting resources, go to Empire, Belief, and Power > Christianity and Medieval Christendom > Christianity's Spread > Explore > Disciples Spread the Story.

Criteria:	Who?	How/Why?
Spreading Christianity		
Converting to Christianity		
Opposing Christianity		

© Discovery Education | www.DiscoveryEducation.com

Name _____ **Date** _____

GRAPHIC ORGANIZER: Venn Diagram

Use this Venn Diagram to compare and contrast the Eastern Orthodox Church and the Roman Catholic Church. For supporting resources, go to Empire, Belief, and Power > Christianity and Medieval Christendom > Christianity's Spread > Explore > The Church Splits.

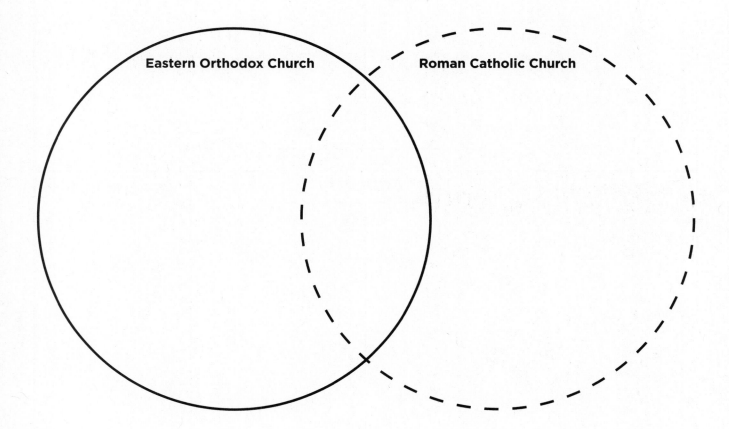

Eastern Orthodox Church

Roman Catholic Church

Name _____ Date _____

GRAPHIC ORGANIZER: Vocabulary Chart

Use this Vocabulary Chart to define the word *schism*. For supporting resources, go to Empire, Belief, and Power > Christianity and Medieval Christendom > Christianity's Spread > Explore > The Church Splits.

DEFINITION:

Personal:

Dictionary:

EXAMPLES (Drawn or Written):

TERM:
schism

SENTENCES:
Teacher/Book:

Personal:

RELATED:

WORD PARTS:

Outside of School (Who Would Use the Word? How Would He or She Use It?):

Name _____ Date _____

EXPLORE: FOCUS QUESTIONS

Using what you learned from the Core Interactive Text, answer each page's focus question:

Disciples Spread the Story
Who spread Christianity after Jesus died?

_____

_____

_____

Suffering for Beliefs
How and why were Christians persecuted for their beliefs?

_____

_____

_____

The Emperor Constantine Adopts Christianity
How did Constantine influence Christianity?

_____

_____

_____

Monks and Monasteries Help Christianity Expand
How did monks help Christianity grow into the world's largest religion?

_____

_____

_____

Christianity Spreads After the Empire Falls
How did the fall of the Roman Empire affect Christianity?

_____

_____

_____

The Church Splits
How did the East-West Schism lead to two separate Christian churches?

_____

_____

_____

PROJECTS AND ASSESSMENTS

Explain Activities

ACTIVITY TYPE: DIAGRAM

Spread of Christianity

In the main idea web, identify three factors that led to the spread of Christianity throughout the Roman Empire and other parts of Europe.

ACTIVITY TYPE: YOU AS JOURNALIST

Christianity's Spread

In this activity, you will write an article that follows one of these headlines: "Little-Known Religion of Christianity Now Spreading Throughout the Empire," "Religion Spreads Despite Persecution," or "Emperor Embraces New Faith."

ACTIVITY TYPE: SOCIAL STUDIES EXPLANATION

Christianity's Spread

In this Social Studies Explanation activity, you will use a template to assemble evidence from the sources you have explored. Then, you will write an answer to the Essential Question and defend your answer with supporting evidence.

Elaborate Activities

photo: Getty Images

INVESTIGATION TYPE: TIMELINE MAP

A New Religion Takes Wing

How did Christianity become the most common religion in medieval Europe? In this investigation, you will use the Timeline Map interactive tool to examine how Christianity grew from a small Middle Eastern sect to one of the most widespread religions in the medieval world.

photo: Getty Images

ACTIVITY TYPE: CURRENT EVENTS CONNECTION

Christianity: Past and Present

In this activity, you will consider the issues that resulted in the schism between the Eastern and Western Christian churches in 1054 CE.

PROJECTS AND ASSESSMENTS *(continued)*

photo: Library of Congress

ACTIVITY TYPE: ROLE PLAY

Early Monks: Their Life and Legacy

In this activity, you will work with a partner to prepare an interview in which you will take turns role-playing the interviewer and interview subject.

photo: Getty Images

ACTIVITY TYPE: DOCUMENT-BASED INVESTIGATION

Christianity's Spread

In this Document-Based Investigation, you will analyze source materials and investigate this question: What role did women play in the spread of Christianity in the Roman Empire?

Evaluate Activities

BRIEF-CONSTRUCTED RESPONSE (BCR)

Christianity's Spread

EXTENDED-CONSTRUCTED RESPONSE (ECR)

Christianity's Spread

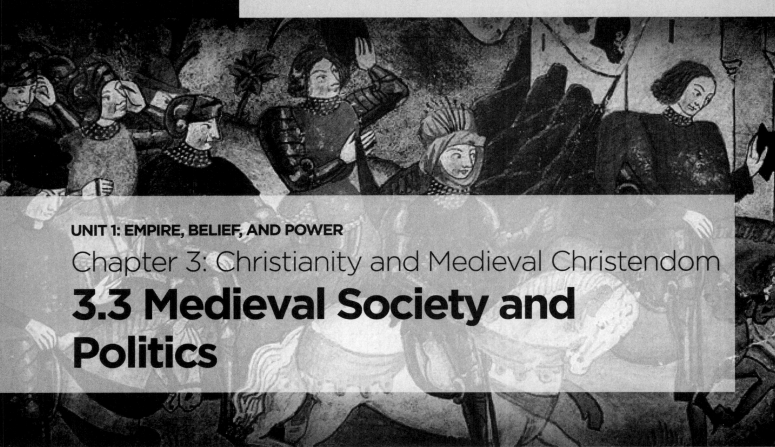

UNIT 1: EMPIRE, BELIEF, AND POWER

Chapter 3: Christianity and Medieval Christendom

3.3 Medieval Society and Politics

photo: Getty Images

LESSON OVERVIEW

Lesson Objectives:

By the end of this lesson, you should be able to:

- **Describe social structures during the Middle Ages, including feudalism and manorialism.**
- **Explain the emergence of nation-states (France, England, Spain, Russia) and their political structures.**
- **Analyze the effects of various conflicts (i.e., Crusades, Mongol conquests, fall of Constantinople) among Eurasian powers.**

Lesson Essential Question:

How did power and social class impact life in medieval Europe?

Key Vocabulary

agriculture, Byzantine Empire, Charlemagne, chivalry, citadel, civil war, conscription, Crusaders / Crusades, Diocletian, Egypt, England, English Bill of Rights, Europe, feudalism, fief, France, Genghis Khan, goods, guild, Hundred Years' War, Israel, Istanbul, Joan of Arc, King Ferdinand, King John of England, knight, lord, Magna Carta, manor, manorialism, Mediterranean Sea, merchant, Middle Ages, monarch, monarchy, Mongols, nation-state, Normandy, Queen Isabella, Renaissance, Roman Empire, Rome, serf, socialism, Spain, Syria, trade, tsar / czar, vassal, William of Normandy

FLASHCARDS

1 Feudalism and Manorialism During the Middle Ages

During the Middle Ages in Europe, the military and political system of feudalism and the economic system of manorialism developed.

- Feudalism was based on a system of a lord granting land to a vassal in return for services.
- Lords and vassals offered land to professional soldiers called knights, who in return pledged to defend the lords.
- Feudalism produced a social system divided into four classes: kings, nobles and church officials, knights, and peasants.
- Knights followed a code of behavior called chivalry.
- Peasants worked the land for their lord and had few rights.
- Manorialism was a self-sufficient economic system in which the lord of an estate lived in a manor house and peasants worked his land.
- Many peasants were serfs—people who were bound to their lord's estate and had to farm their lord's land in addition to their own land.

Why Does It Matter?

Feudalism and manorialism helped improve the economic condition of Europe in the Middle Ages, helping to set the scene for the rise of powerful kingdoms. Feudalism also developed a judicial system that strongly affected modern jury systems.

photo: The New York Public Library
This photograph shows a castle and nearby gardens in the spring.

2 England, France, Spain, and Russia Form Stronger Kingdoms

The monarchs of England, France, Spain, and Russia formed stronger kingdoms, which eventually developed into nation-states.

- During the High Middle Ages, many kings obtained more money, thereby enabling them to form a strong army, gain more power over lords, and expand their kingdoms.
- The Norman lord, William the Conqueror, conquered the Anglo-Saxons and established a strong central government in England. Kings gained power until nobles and church officials forced King John to sign the Magna Carta.
- Louis IX strengthened the central government of France.
- The Christian Spanish drove the Muslims out of Spain. Prince Ferdinand of Aragon married Queen Isabella of Castile, thereby uniting the two kingdoms of Spain.
- Ivan IV became the first tsar of Russia after the Mongols were driven out.

Why Does It Matter?

Efforts to limit the power of lords during the Middle Ages gave rise to the Magna Carta. The Magna Carta has become a model for people who want to establish a democratic government. However, it did not prevent kingdoms from gaining strength. The strong kingdoms established by medieval monarchs developed into modern nations, such as Great Britain, France, Spain, and Russia.

photo: Getty Images
Created around 1390 by an unknown painter, this picture shows King Richard II of England.

FLASHCARDS *(continued)*

3 The Crusades and the Hundred Years' War

The Crusades and the Hundred Years' War had a strong cultural and political impact on Europe.

- **The Crusades—a series of military expeditions by European Christians to gain control of the Holy Land—took place from the early 1000s to the late 1200s.**
- **The Crusades failed to achieve their goal, but they had a strong impact on the society of Europe and relations between Christians and Muslims.**
- **The Hundred Years' War—a series of conflicts between the English and French for control of France—raged on and off from 1337 to 1453.**
- **New weapons like the longbow and cannons helped England win the battles of Crecy and Agincourt during the Hundred Years' War, ultimately led to French victory, and also contributed to the decline of feudalism.**

Why Does It Matter?

The Crusades developed trade with lands beyond Europe and, as a result, encouraged the spread of ideas that later influenced the Renaissance. The long-lasting Byzantine Empire defended Europe from Muslim invasion for hundreds of years. This happened during a time when Europe was fragmented and vulnerable to invasion. The Hundred Years' War contributed to the end of feudalism and the development of nation-states.

EDINBURGH CASTLE, AS IT WAS BEFORE THE SIEGE OF 1573.

photo: The New York Public Library

This illustration shows Edinburgh Castle before the Siege of 1873.

Name _____ **Date** _____

GRAPHIC ORGANIZER: Main Idea Web

Use this Main Idea Web to help you define the vocabulary word *feudalism*. For supporting resources, go to Empire, Belief, and Power > Christianity and Medieval Christendom > Medieval Society and Politics > Explore > The Feudal System.

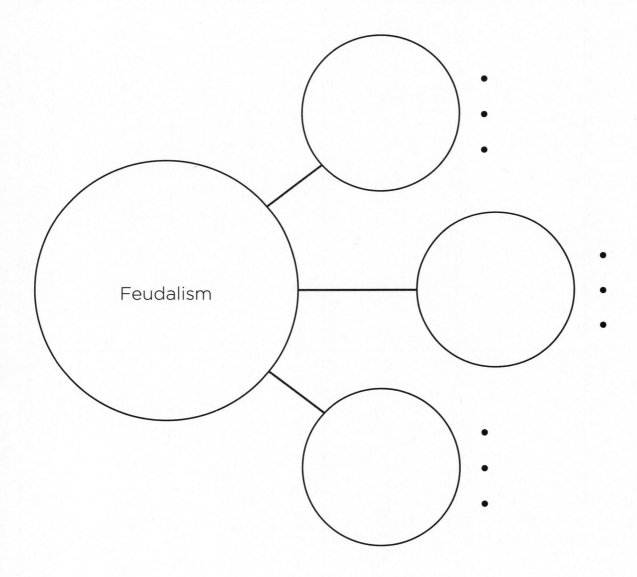

Feudalism

Name _____ **Date** _____

GRAPHIC ORGANIZER: Comparison Chart

Use this Comparison Chart to help you compare and contrast the kingdoms of England, France, Spain, and Russia. For supporting resources, go to Empire, Belief, and Power > Christianity and Medieval Christendom > Medieval Society and Politics > Explore > England.

Nation-State	Leader	Characteristics of Government	Events in the Kingdom's Development
England			
France			

Name _____ **Date** _____

GRAPHIC ORGANIZER: Comparison Chart *(continued)*

Nation-State	Leader	Characteristics of Government	Events in the Kingdom's Development
Spain			
Russia			

Name _____ **Date** _____

GRAPHIC ORGANIZER: Cause/Event/Effect Chart

Use this Cause/Event/Effect Chart to list events related to the Crusades. For each event listed, identify the causes and effects. For supporting resources, go to Empire, Belief, and Power > Christianity and Medieval Christendom > Medieval Society and Politics > Explore > The Beginning of the Crusades.

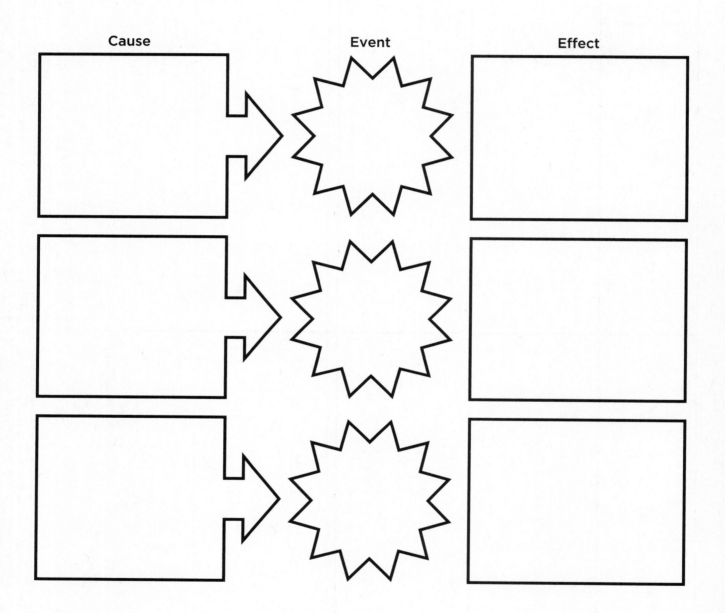

Cause   Event   Effect

Name _____ **Date** _____

GRAPHIC ORGANIZER: Cause/Event/Effect Chart *(continued)*

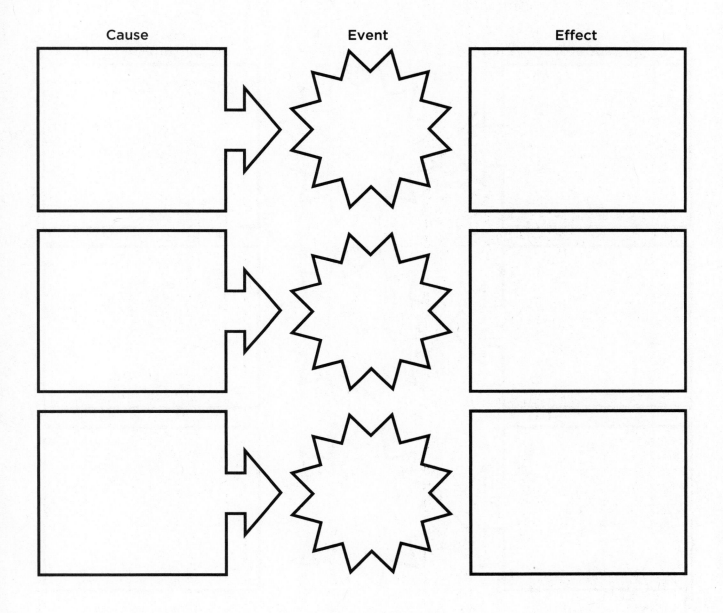

Cause   Event   Effect

Name _____ **Date** _____

GRAPHIC ORGANIZER: Cause/Event/Effect Chart

Use this Cause/Event/Effect chart to list events related to the Hundred Years' War. For each event listed, identify the causes and effects. For supporting resources, go to Empire, Belief, and Power > Christianity and Medieval Christendom > Medieval Society and Politics > Explore > Hundred Years' War.

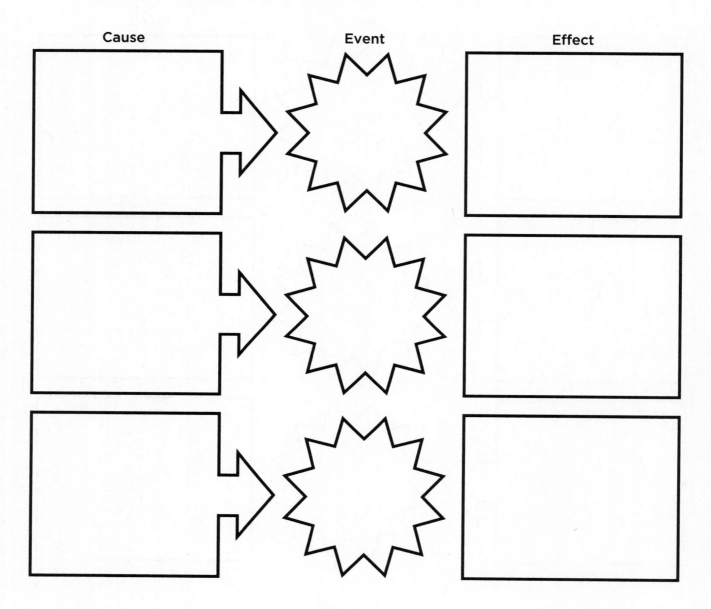

Cause

Event

Effect

Name _____ **Date** _____

GRAPHIC ORGANIZER: Cause/Event/Effect Chart *(continued)*

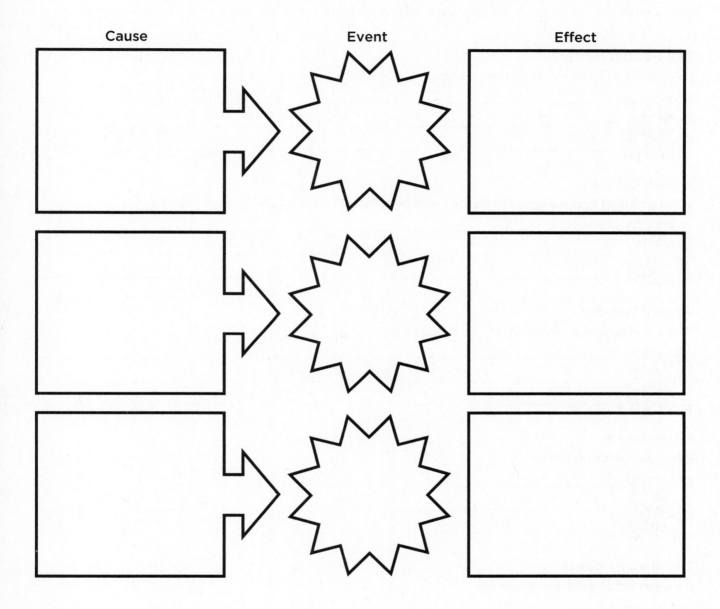

Cause   Event   Effect

Name _____ Date _____

EXPLORE: FOCUS QUESTIONS

Using what you learned from the Core Interactive Text, answer each page's focus question:

The Feudal System
How did the fall of Rome impact Europe?

_____
_____
_____

A New System
What political system arose in Europe after the fall of the Western Roman Empire?

_____
_____
_____

Feudal Society
What was feudal society like in the Middle Ages?

_____
_____
_____

Manorialism
What was manorialism?

_____
_____
_____

The Rise of Kings
How did kings gain more power?

_____
_____
_____

England
How did the kingdom of England develop?

_____
_____
_____

Name _____ Date _____

EXPLORE: FOCUS QUESTIONS *(continued)*

The Great Charter
What is the Magna Carta?

_____
_____
_____

France
How did the kingdom of France develop?

_____
_____
_____

Spain
How did the kingdom of Spain develop?

_____
_____
_____

Russia
How did the kingdom of Russia develop?

_____
_____
_____

Growing Power of the Church
How did religious power and political power overlap in medieval Europe?

_____
_____
_____

The Beginning of the Crusades
What were the Crusades?

_____
_____
_____

Name _____ Date _____

EXPLORE: FOCUS QUESTIONS *(continued)*

The End of the Crusades
What were the major events of the third and fourth Crusades?

_____
_____
_____

Hundred Years' War
What was the Hundred Years' War?

_____
_____
_____

The End of the Wars
How did the Hundred Years' War end?

_____
_____
_____

PROJECTS AND ASSESSMENTS

Explain Activities

ACTIVITY TYPE: DIAGRAM

Medieval Society and Politics
In this activity, you will use a word bank to create a graphic explanation of feudalism.

ACTIVITY TYPE: VISUALIZATION

Power in the Middle Ages
In this activity, you will sketch out story ideas for a TV miniseries that focuses on the Middle Ages.

ACTIVITY TYPE: SOCIAL STUDIES EXPLANATION

Medieval Society and Politics
In this Social Studies Explanation activity, you will use a template to assemble evidence from the sources you have explored. Then, you will write an answer to the Essential Question and defend your answer with supporting evidence.

Elaborate Activities

photo: Discovery Education

INVESTIGATION TYPE: HISTORICAL PERSPECTIVES

Medieval Society
Your mission is to get to know four individuals who might have lived in medieval Europe and explore the perspectives each would have had on key issues of the day.

photo: Library of Congress

ACTIVITY TYPE: PITCH YOUR IDEA

Bid for Manor Construction
For this activity, you will work either as an architect to design a layout for a manor or as a contractor to create a construction proposal.

PROJECTS AND ASSESSMENTS *(continued)*

photo: Discovery Education

ACTIVITY TYPE: EXPRESS YOUR OPINION

The Magna Carta

In this activity, you will write a letter—as James Madison—in response to a friend's letter asking if there is a particular document that has especially shaped your ideas about government. In the letter, you will explain that the Magna Carta influenced your ideas about government.

photo: Getty Images

ACTIVITY TYPE: DOCUMENT-BASED INVESTIGATION

Medieval Society and Politics

In this Document-Based Investigation, you will analyze source materials and investigate this question: In his book *Everything There is to Know about Medieval History*, Professor Know-It-All wrote: "Feudalism was an oppressive system, which trapped people in social classes and gave them no rights or protections." Do you agree with Professor Know-It-All? What rights and obligations did different groups have in medieval society?

photo: IRC

ACTIVITY TYPE: DOCUMENT-BASED INVESTIGATION

Medieval Society and Politics

In this activity, you will analyze the factors that led to the rise of the kings of England. You will write a report or create a museum exhibit for the historical society.

Evaluate Activities

BRIEF-CONSTRUCTED RESPONSE (BCR)

Medieval Society and Politics

EXTENDED-CONSTRUCTED RESPONSE (ECR)

Medieval Society and Politics

UNIT 1: EMPIRE, BELIEF, AND POWER

Chapter 3: Christianity and Medieval Christendom
3.4 The Black Death

photo: Getty Images

LESSON OVERVIEW

Lesson Objectives:

By the end of this lesson, you should be able to:

- Describe the Black Death and its effect on Eurasia and the world.
- Identify patterns related to the spread and recovery of people suffering from the Black Death.

Key Vocabulary

Black Plague / Black Death (bubonic plague), epidemic, Europe, feudalism, flagellants, Mediterranean Sea, Mongols

Lesson Essential Question:

How did the Black Death spark social, political, and economic change throughout Europe?

FLASHCARDS

1 The Black Death Spread Quickly

Once rooted in Europe, the Black Death spread quickly and efficiently through the population.

- **The plague came to Europe and the Middle East from China through trade routes.**
- **Fleas and infected rats spread the disease throughout the city and countryside.**
- **Certain hygiene practices helped the bubonic plague spread quickly.**

Why Does It Matter?

The Black Death is a reminder of the vulnerability of humans to diseases and viruses. Today, the world is highly interconnected through trade. Small animals and insects carry disease, and in many parts of the world, substandard hygienic practices threaten the health of the population. These factors make it possible for an outbreak similar to the Black Death to explode across our world.

photo: Getty's Open Content Program
This painting from the 1700s shows a monk praying for plague victims in the 1300s.

2 The Black Death Changed Europe and Asia

The Black Death ravaged Europe and Asia, leading to economic, political, and social changes.

- **The Black Death is the nickname for the bubonic plague, which killed millions of people throughout the world.**
- **The Black Death reappeared about every 10 years throughout the 1400s and 1500s.**
- **The Black Death changed people's views on religion. Some, such as the flagellants, viewed it as a punishment from God and became more devout. Others lost faith in God based on the disaster and began to turn to science for answers.**
- **The depopulation of Europe led to a labor shortage.**
- **Because workers were in greater demand, they began to receive higher wages.**
- **An increase in wages led to inflated prices for everyday goods.**
- **Landowners were forced to pay wages to keep their tenants, leading to an increase in wealth in the peasant class.**
- **Many serfs left their manors for better jobs in the city.**
- **The increase in wealth and opportunity for the lower classes led to a new social mobility that, combined with the decreased population, led to a decline in feudalism.**

Why Does It Matter?

The Black Death reduced the population of Europe by approximately one-third. It reached all classes of society. The resulting labor shortage led to growth of towns and cities and the end of the feudal system, as serfs began to receive wages for their work.

photo: Corbis
The Black Death reached everywhere. In this woodcut, Londoners flee the city to avoid the plague.

Name _____ **Date** _____

GRAPHIC ORGANIZER: GREASES Chart

Use this GREASES chart to discuss the characteristics of European society before, during, and after the Black Death. For supporting resources, go to Empire, Belief, and Power > Christianity and Medieval Christendom > The Black Death > Explore > The Plague Begins.

Government	
Religion	
Economic	
Art & Architecture	
Science & Technology	
Environment	
Social & Cultural Values	

Name _____ Date _____

GRAPHIC ORGANIZER: Cause/Effect Chart

Use this Cause/Event Chart to describe the three main causes of the spread of the Black Death and their effects on society during this time. For supporting resources, go to Empire, Belief, and Power > Christianity and Medieval Christendom > The Black Death > Explore > The Black Death Transforms Society.

Cause   **Effect**

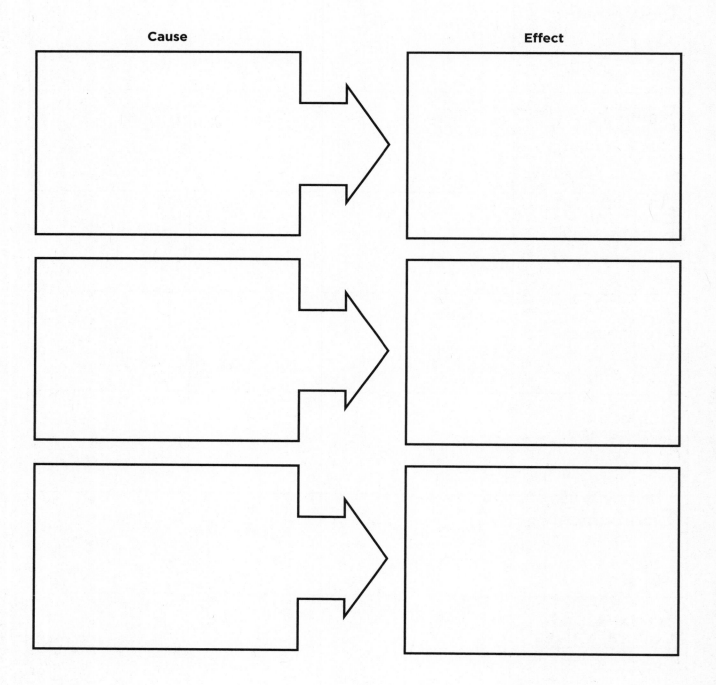

Name _____ Date _____

EXPLORE: FOCUS QUESTIONS

Using what you learned from the Core Interactive Text, answer each page's focus question:

The Plague Begins
What was the origin of the bubonic plague?

_____

_____

_____

The Black Death Spreads Across Europe
How did the Black Death spread through Europe?

_____

_____

_____

Living Conditions Assist the Spread of the Black Death
How did hygiene practices help spread the Black Death?

_____

_____

_____

The Black Death Transforms Society
What social changes resulted from the Black Death?

_____

_____

_____

Europe Depopulates
How did a reduction in population affect European economics?

_____

_____

_____

Political Impact of the Black Death
How did a reduction in population affect European politics?

_____

_____

_____

PROJECTS AND ASSESSMENTS

Explain Activities

ACTIVITY TYPE: YOU AS JOURNALIST

After the Bubonic Plague

In this You as Journalist activity, you will write a news article describing the effects of the Black Death on the economic, social, or political characteristics of Europe.

ACTIVITY TYPE: DIAGRAM

Impact of the Black Death

In this activity, you will use at least 10 words from the word bank to create a graphic answer to the Essential Question.

ACTIVITY TYPE: SOCIAL STUDIES EXPLANATION

The Black Death

In this Social Studies Explanation activity, you will use a template to assemble evidence from the sources you have explored. Then, you will write an answer to the Essential Question and defend your answer with supporting evidence.

Elaborate Activities

photo: National Gallery of Art

INVESTIGATION TYPE: TIMELINE MAP

Black Death

How did the Black Death spread, and what effects did it have throughout Europe? In this investigation, you will use the Timeline Map interactive tool to explain how the Black Death came to Europe and affected people there.

photo: Getty Images

ACTIVITY TYPE: ROLE PLAY

Life During the Black Death

In this activity, you will imagine that you are living in the city of Florence, Italy, during a plague outbreak.

PROJECTS AND ASSESSMENTS *(continued)*

photo: Getty Images

ACTIVITY TYPE: CURRENT EVENTS CONNECTION

Modern Epidemics

In this activity, you will research how the effects of more recent disease epidemics compare to the effects of the Black Death.

photo: Getty Images

ACTIVITY TYPE: DOCUMENT-BASED INVESTIGATION

The Black Death

In this Document-Based Investigation, you will analyze source materials and investigate this question: How did the Black Death affect European society?

Evaluate Activities

BRIEF-CONSTRUCTED RESPONSE (BCR)

Black Death

EXTENDED-CONSTRUCTED RESPONSE (ECR)

Black Death

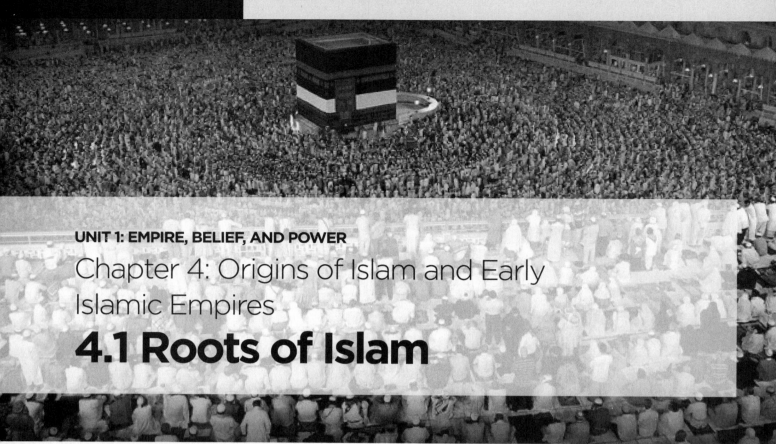

UNIT 1: EMPIRE, BELIEF, AND POWER

Chapter 4: Origins of Islam and Early Islamic Empires

4.1 Roots of Islam

LESSON OVERVIEW

Lesson Objectives:

By the end of this lesson, you should be able to:

- Describe how the geography of the Arabian Peninsula shaped the way of life of the people living there.
- Identify Muhammad, his teachings, and his contributions to the growth of Islam in Asia.
- Describe the origins and characteristics of Islam.
- Explain the importance of the Quran to culture and politics in the Islamic world.

Lesson Essential Question:

How did Islam develop?

Key Vocabulary

Abu Bakr, Ali, Arabia, Arabian Peninsula, Arabian Sea, Bedouin, beginning of Islam, caravan, desert, Egyptians, Five Pillars of Islam, imam, Indian Ocean, Islam, Kaaba, Mecca, Medina, merchant, Mesopotamia, Middle East, monotheism, mosque, Muhammad, Muslims, nomadic, oasis, peninsula, Persian Gulf, polytheism, Quran, Red Sea, Shariah, Shi'a Islam, Southwest Asia, Sunnah, trade, Yemen

FLASHCARDS

1 Deserts and Mountains

Islam began in the Arabian Peninsula. The peninsula is hot and mostly dry. It contains deserts, oases, mountains, and a narrow strip of fertile coastland along the edge.

- Desert covers three-fourths of the Arabian Peninsula. The desert contains large expanses of sand dunes but also dry plains and plateaus. People who live in the desert live nomadic lives, traveling from oasis to oasis in search of water for their livestock.

- Oases, or areas where freshwater is available, dot the desert. Over time, some nomads settled in oases and began to farm. Some oases also became trading centers.

- Mountains cover the western and southeastern sections of the Arabian Peninsula. The climate is somewhat cooler and wetter in the mountains, allowing farming to occur.

- A strip of fertile coastland hugs the edges of the Arabian Peninsula. This area receives enough rain that farming is possible. Trade centers also developed in areas with natural harbors.

- The Arabian Peninsula has many trade routes that merchants used as they traveled between the civilizations of the Mediterranean Sea and those of the Indian Ocean.

Why Does It Matter?

The geography of the Arabian Peninsula influenced the development of Islam and its spread to other areas.

photo: Library of Congress

An oasis appears in the middle of the desert.

2 Muhammad: the Final Prophet

Muslims believe Muhammad was the final prophet of Islam.

- Muhammad was born around 570 in the trading city of Mecca. He became a trader and married Khadijah, a wealthy merchant from Mecca.

- When Muhammad was about 40, he is believed to have received a revelation from God. Over the next 22 years, he continued to receive revelations.

- Muhammad preached belief in the one God and fair treatment of the poor and others without power. Meccan elites did not like his message, which threatened their wealth and power. They actively worked against Muhammad and his followers.

- In 622, Muhammad and his followers left Mecca to live in the city of Medina. Medinans converted to Islam, and Islam spread throughout the Arabian Peninsula. In 630, Muhammad and his followers reentered Mecca, destroyed the idols, and rededicated the Kaaba to Islam.

- Muhammad died in 632 after his second pilgrimage to Mecca.

Why Does It Matter?

Muhammad founded the religion of Islam. Today, many Muslims follow in Muhammad's footsteps by making a pilgrimage to Mecca.

photo: Bigstock

Before Muhammad rededicated the Kaaba to God, it housed the idols of thousands of local gods. The Kaaba is central to Islam.

FLASHCARDS *(continued)*

3 **The Beliefs and Practices of Islam**

Muslims follow five core practices, called the Five Pillars of Islam. They also use the Quran and the Sunnah to guide their actions.

- The first pillar of Islam is faith. Muslims must proclaim that they believe in one God and that Muhammad is his prophet.

- The second pillar of Islam is prayer. Muslims pray five times a day, facing Mecca.

- The third pillar of Islam is charity. Muslims are required to give a percentage of their income and possessions to the poor.

- The fourth pillar of Islam is fasting. During the month of Ramadan, Muslims fast from sunrise to sundown.

- The fifth pillar of Islam is pilgrimage. All Muslims who are able are required to make the pilgrimage to Mecca at least once in their lifetime.

- The Quran is the holy book of Islam. It contains the revelations that Muhammad is said to have received from God through the angel Gabriel. It is the primary source of guidance for all Muslims.

- The Sunnah is a collection of stories about the sayings and doings of Muhammad. Muslims use these stories as guidance when the Quran does not guide them on how to act.

Why Does It Matter?

The Five Pillars of Islam and the teachings in the Quran and the Sunnah form the core of the Islamic faith.

photo: Jupiterimages Corporation

The Quran is the collection of the series of revelations Muhammad is said to have received from God.

Name _____ Date _____

GRAPHIC ORGANIZER: Roots of Islam: Map

Use this Map to label and describe the geographic characteristics of the region. For supporting resources, go to Empire, Belief, and Power > Origins of Islam and Early Islamic Empires > Roots of Islam > Explore > The Birthplace of Islam.

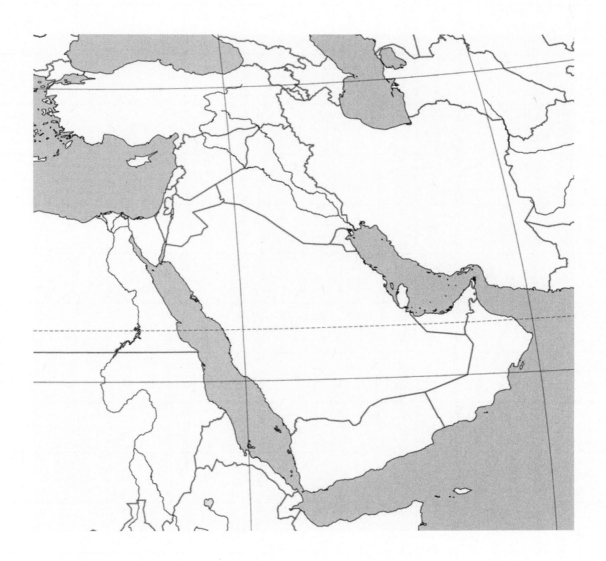

Name _____**Date** _____

GRAPHIC ORGANIZER: Roots of Islam: Map *(continued)*

Geographic Feature	Definition/Description

Name _____ **Date** _____

GRAPHIC ORGANIZER: Sequencing Chart

Use this Sequencing Chart to list at least 10 significant events in Muhammad's life and their importance to the founding of Islam in chronological order. For supporting resources, go to Empire, Belief, and Power > Origins of Islam and Early Islamic Empires > Roots of Islam > Explore > Muhammad—the Trader.

Event	Date	Summary

Name _____ **Date** _____

GRAPHIC ORGANIZER: Sequencing Chart *(continued)*

Event	Date	Summary

Name _____**Date** _____

GRAPHIC ORGANIZER: Main Idea Web

Use this Main Idea Web to record information about Islam's five core practices. For supporting resources, go to Empire, Belief, and Power > Origins of Islam and Early Islamic Empires > Roots of Islam > Explore > Faith, Prayer, Charity, Fasting, and Pilgrimage.

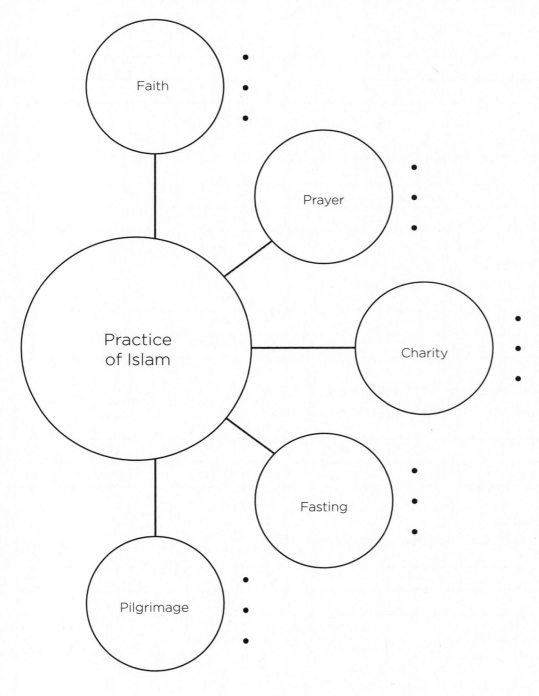

Name _____ Date _____

EXPLORE: FOCUS QUESTIONS

Using what you learned from the Core Interactive Text, answer each page's focus question:

The Birthplace of Islam
Where did Islam begin?

_____
_____
_____
_____

Deserts and Nomads
How did the geography of the Arabian Peninsula shape life there?

_____
_____
_____
_____

Muhammad—the Trader
How did Muhammad begin to teach the religion of Islam?

_____
_____
_____
_____

The Revelations and Teachings of Muhammad
What message did Muhammad spread to the people of Mecca?

_____
_____
_____
_____

Reaction and Resistance
How did the people of Mecca react to Muhammad's message?

_____
_____
_____
_____

Name _____ Date _____

EXPLORE: FOCUS QUESTIONS *(continued)*

Faith, Prayer, Charity, Fasting, and Pilgrimage
What are Muslims required to do?

_____

_____

_____

A Holy Book and Guides to Follow
Where do Muslims receive guidance for how to live their lives?

_____

_____

_____

PROJECTS AND ASSESSMENTS

Explain Activities

ACTIVITY TYPE: VISUALIZATION

The Development of Islam

How did the Islamic religion develop over time? Draw or find and paste illustrations in the story frames that show events in the story of Islam. On the lines beneath each frame, describe each event in the development of Islam and explain its significance.

ACTIVITY TYPE: DIAGRAM

Four Religions

In this activity, you will use a comparison chart to describe the aspects of Judaism, Christianity, Islam, and another religion of your choice. Then, you will write a paragraph comparing and contrasting elements of the four religions.

ACTIVITY TYPE: SOCIAL STUDIES EXPLANATION

Roots of Islam

In this Social Studies Explanation activity, you will use a template to assemble evidence from the sources you have explored. Then, you will write an answer to the Essential Question and defend your answer with supporting evidence.

Elaborate Activities

 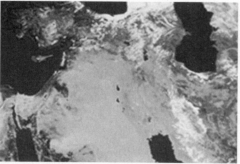

photo: Getty Images

INVESTIGATION TYPE: MAP-GUIDED INQUIRY

Roots of Islam

How did geography influence the development of Islam? In this investigation, you will use the Map-Guided Inquiry interactive tool to examine the development and growth of Islam in the region of the Arabian Peninsula.

photo: Getty Images

ACTIVITY TYPE: SAY WHAT?

The Quran: The Story of Noah

In this activity, you will read an excerpt from the Quran describing Noah's experiences during the Great Flood and translate it for modern times. Then, you will respond to the analysis questions.

PROJECTS AND ASSESSMENTS *(continued)*

photo: Getty Images

ACTIVITY TYPE: DOCUMENT-BASED
INVESTIGATION

Roots of Islam

In this Document-Based Investigation, you
will examine the sources and investigate this
question: Is monotheism the only common
element of Christianity, Judaism, and Islam?

Evaluate Activities

BRIEF-CONSTRUCTED RESPONSE (BCR)

Roots of Islam

EXTENDED-CONSTRUCTED RESPONSE (ECR)

Roots of Islam

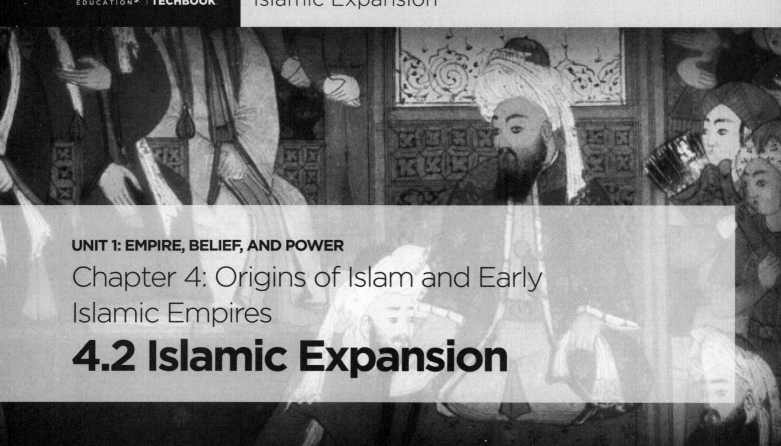

UNIT 1: EMPIRE, BELIEF, AND POWER

Chapter 4: Origins of Islam and Early Islamic Empires

4.2 Islamic Expansion

LESSON OVERVIEW

Lesson Objectives:

By the end of this lesson, you should be able to:

- Identify important figures and then analyze their significance to the development, spread, and division of Islam.

- Trace Islamic expansion throughout Asia and Africa as a result of military conquests and unprepared adversaries.

- Describe the encounters between Muslims and Christians during the expansion of the Islamic world.

Key Vocabulary

Abbasid dynasty, Abu Bakr, annex, astrolabe, Byzantine Empire, caliph, caliphate, Crusaders / Crusades, Egypt, First Fitna, heretic, imam, Iraq, Islam, jihad, Mecca, Medina, Mesopotamia, Mombasa, Moors, Morocco, Muhammad, People of the Book, Quran, Rashidun caliphate, Riddah Wars, Sassanid Empire, Shi'a Islam, Southwest Asia, Spain, subcontinent, Sunnah, Sunni Islam, Syria, Umar, Umayyad dynasty, ummah, Uthman

Lesson Essential Question:

What factors led to the rapid growth of Islam around Africa, Asia, and Eastern Europe?

FLASHCARDS

1 ▸ The Power of the Word

Over the years, Islam expanded from a local religion to a national religion to a regional religion and finally a world religion. A great number of important individuals helped Islam through each stage, right up to the present day. Without the early personalities of the Rashidun Caliphate, however, Islam would not have spread.

- Abu Bakr united the Arabian Peninsula under Islam.
- Caliph Umar expanded the empire to include Egypt, Iran, and parts of Turkey.
- During the reign of the early caliphs, Muslim scholars compiled the teachings of Muhammad into a single work, known as the Quran, written in Arabic. The Quran contributed to the sense of common identity that developed first among Arabs and later among other cultures.
- Ali, Muhammad's cousin and son-in-law, was a Rashidun, or "rightly guided" caliph. Some Muslims believe he should have been the first heir to Muhammad's religious and political power; others do not. This conflict caused the split of Islam into the Sunni and Shi'a branches.

Why Does It Matter?

Islam would not have spread if the Arab people had not achieved a sense of unity. However, the expansion of the early Islamic Empire led to internal tensions over political leadership. These tensions laid the foundation for the split between Sunni and Shi'a branches of Islam that continues to the present day.

photo: Library of Congress

The Mosque of Umar in Jerusalem is the third most holy site in the Islamic religion.

2 ▸ Peace for All Nations

Muslims worked out a fairly peaceful relationship with Christians and Jews during the first 500 years of expansion. This relationship avoided religious-based conflicts between the Islamic rulers and the non-Muslims they ruled.

- Jews and Christians were, like Muslims, "People of the Book" who followed many of the same prophets and shared many of the same beliefs.
- The Constitution of Medina (about 622) spelled out the rights and responsibilities that Jews and Christians had in the ummah.
- By becoming dhimmis under Muslim rule and paying the special taxes, Christians and Jews were able to maintain many of their traditions and culture.

Why Does It Matter?

Non-Muslims had a place under Muslim rule during the first 500 years. Although they were not considered equal, they were not terrorized or persecuted the way groups of non-Christians were in Europe.

photo: Getty Images

Muslims and Christians generally lived together in peace under Muslim rule, but eventually tension built and led to conflict.

FLASHCARDS *(continued)*

3 ### The Further Expansion of Islam

The expansion of Islam and the expansion of Muslim rule throughout Asia and Africa were two different processes.

- Muslim armies made countless conquests, first under the Arabs and later under a plethora of other cultural groups such as the Persians, the Berbers, and the Turks.

- Islam expanded at its own pace. In some cultures it was accepted fairly quickly; in others it took up to 400 years. Because it was rarely forced on people, conversion often became a practical decision made by people who lived under Muslim rule for generations.

Why Does It Matter?

The issue of expansion is bigger than some people think. Islam as a religion did not spread by the sword; Muslim rule did.

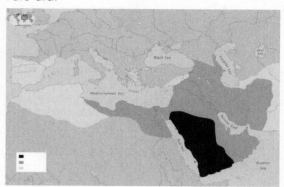

photo: Discovery Education

Islam expanded from the Arabian Peninsula to other parts of Southeast Asia, North Africa, and Europe from 622 to 733.

Name _____ **Date** _____

GRAPHIC ORGANIZER: Sequencing Chart

Use this Sequencing Chart to list significant events in the expansion of Islam in chronological order. For supporting resources, go to Empire, Belief, and Power > Origins of Islam and Early Islamic Empires > Islamic Expansion > Explore > Arab Unity or Separation?

Event	Date	Summary

Name _____**Date** _____

GRAPHIC ORGANIZER: Sequencing Chart *(continued)*

Event	Date	Summary

Name _____**Date** _____

GRAPHIC ORGANIZER: Cause/Event/Effect Chart

Use this Cause/Event/Effect Chart to record the causes and effects of the Crusades. For supporting resources, go to Empire, Belief, and Power > Origins of Islam and Early Islamic Empires > Islamic Expansion > Explore > The Crusades.

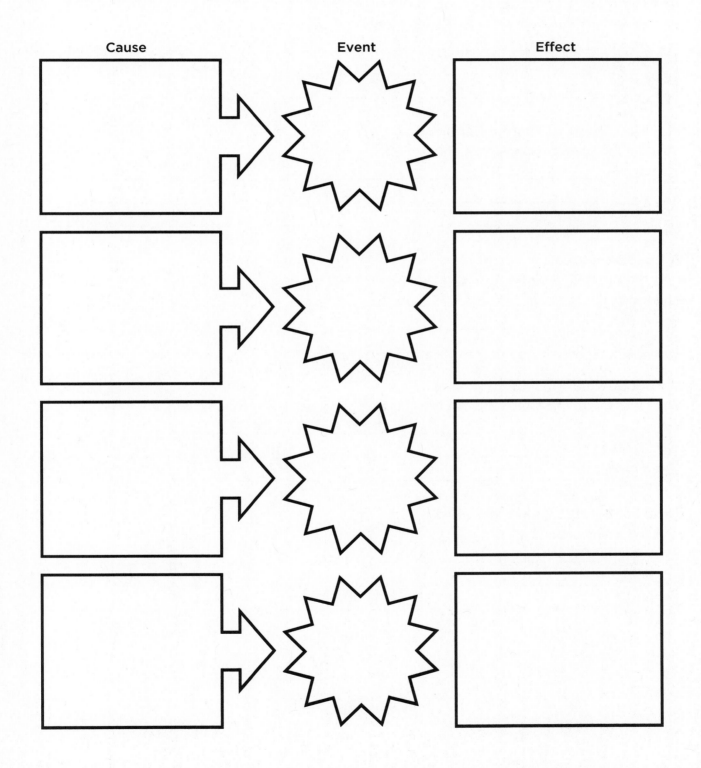

Name _____ Date _____

EXPLORE: FOCUS QUESTIONS

Using what you learned from the Core Interactive Text, answer each page's focus question:

Arab Unity or Separation?

How important was Arab unity to Islamic expansion?

_____

_____

_____

The First Wave of Islamic Expansion

How did the Islamic expansions begin?

_____

_____

_____

A Split Develops

How did the split between Shi'a and Sunni Muslims originate?

_____

_____

_____

A Special Relationship

What was the relationship between Muslims and Christians in the Islamic world?

_____

_____

_____

Time Is Mightier Than the Sword

How did Islam spread?

_____

_____

_____

Name _____ Date _____

EXPLORE: FOCUS QUESTIONS *(continued)*

A World Religion
How did Islam expand after the year 750?

_____
_____
_____

The Crusades
What were the Crusades?

_____
_____
_____

PROJECTS AND ASSESSMENTS

Explain Activities

ACTIVITY TYPE: DIAGRAM

Islamic Expansion: Mind Map

In this Diagram activity, you will use at least 14 words from the word bank to create a Mind Map that answers the Essential Question: What factors led to the rapid growth of Islam around Africa, Asia, and Eastern Europe?

ACTIVITY TYPE: VISUALIZATION

The Rashidun Caliphate

In this Visualization activity, you will use a Story Frames graphic organizer to illustrate and describe the years of the Rashidun Caliphate, the first four Muslim caliphs after Muhammad's death.

ACTIVITY TYPE: SOCIAL STUDIES EXPLANATION

Islamic Expansion

In this Social Studies Explanation activity, you will use a template to assemble evidence from the sources you have explored. Then, you will write an answer to the Essential Question and defend your answer with supporting evidence.

Elaborate Activities

photo: Getty Images

INVESTIGATION TYPE: TIMELINE MAP

The Spread of Islam

What events led to the expansion of the Islamic religion throughout Africa, Asia, and Eastern Europe? In this investigation, you will use the Timeline Map interactive tool to examine the religious and political forces behind the spread of Islam throughout Africa, Asia, and Eastern Europe.

PROJECTS AND ASSESSMENTS *(continued)*

photo: Getty Images

ACTIVITY TYPE: EXPRESS YOUR OPINION

Reasons for Tolerance

In this activity, you will imagine that you are an adviser to a Muslim caliph who is deciding on a policy regarding the practice of other religions in his territory. You will write a letter to the caliph expressing your opinion in support of continuing the policy of tolerance and supporting your opinion with religious, political, and/or economic reasons.

photo: Library of Congress

ACTIVITY TYPE: YOU AS ARTIST

Traveling Through the Muslim World

In this activity, you will read descriptions of an area visited by Benjamin of Tudela, a Jewish traveler of the mid-1100s. Then, you will draw an image of the region he explored and explain what your image shows about life in the Islamic Empire at that time.

photo: Getty Images

ACTIVITY TYPE: DOCUMENT-BASED INVESTIGATION

Islamic Expansion

In this Document-Based Investigation, you will examine the sources and investigate this question: Was military conquest the chief reason for the spread of Islam from 550 to 1450?

Evaluate Activities

BRIEF-CONSTRUCTED RESPONSE (BCR)

Islamic Expansion

EXTENDED-CONSTRUCTED RESPONSE (ECR)

Islamic Expansion

UNIT 1: EMPIRE, BELIEF, AND POWER

Chapter 4: Origins of Islam and Early Islamic Empires

4.3 Life in the Islamic Empires

photo: Getty Images

LESSON OVERVIEW

Lesson Objectives:

By the end of this lesson, you should be able to:

- Explain how the development of trade routes led to the growth of cities and the economy in Islamic society.

- Analyze how the Islamic religion affected life for men and women in the region.

- Connect important innovations under Islamic empires to the expansion of global trade and cultural diffusion.

Lesson Essential Question:

How did trade, religion, and innovation shape society in Islamic cultures?

Key Vocabulary

Abbas the Great, Africa, Arabia, Arabian Peninsula, Arabian Sea, Asia, Byzantine Empire, camel, caravan, Delhi Sultanate, domestication, Europe, Five Pillars of Islam, hijab, Ibn Battuta, India, Indian Subcontinent, Janissaries, Mecca, Medina, Middle East, millets, oasis, patriarchal, pilgrimage, polytheism, Ptolemy, Quran, Red Sea, reform / social reform, shah, Shariah, Spain, sultan, Umar, Uthman

FLASHCARDS

1 Development of Islamic Society

Islamic society developed on the Arabian Peninsula and spread to new places through Muslim traders. Important cities for trade were also important cities for Islamic society.

- **The location of the Arabian Peninsula made it an important place for trade.**
- **Weather patterns and climate had an impact on where, when, and how trade took place.**
- **Two important cities to the development of Islamic society were the trade cities of Mecca and Medina.**
- **Muslim traders shared the Islamic faith with people in new lands along trade routes. This helped Islam and Islamic culture spread.**

Why Does It Matter?

Trade routes were important to the economic and cultural life of cities in the Islamic empires. Islam spread throughout the region along land- and sea-based trade routes.

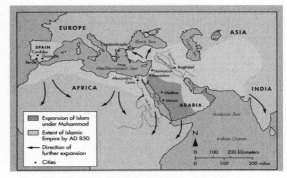

Islam spread from the Arabian Penninsula.

2 Life in Islamic Society

Islamic law gave new rules that affected how Muslim men and women were expected to live. Islamic society became a place where many cultures came together to share ideas.

- **Before Islam, tribes living on the Arabian Peninsula did not give women many rights.**
- **The Quran said that women and men were equal in the eyes of God.**
- **The Quran gave women rights that they did not have in pre-Islamic society.**
- **The Quran gave both women and men rules about how to live their day-to-day lives.**
- **People of other religions were allowed to live and worship freely in many Islamic empires.**
- **Ideas and traditions from across the world came together in the Islamic empires.**

Why Does It Matter?

Because Islam brought people from many different cultures together, people combined many different ideas and world views to make a new culture. This new culture was shaped by Islamic law.

God was at the center of life in Islamic society. Muslims generally pray at home or work and then gather for Friday prayers at the mosque.

FLASHCARDS (continued)

3

Important Innovations of the Muslim Empires

The Islamic empires were a place of scientific study and innovation. The advances made in science, mathematics, and culture affected the way that different parts of the world connected with one another.

- Muslim scholars translated and studied the works of ancient scientists and philosophers from across the world.
- The Islamic empires united a large area with one religion and one language.
- Muslim scholars made advances in navigation, geography, and mathematics in order to fulfill two pillars of Islam, hajj and salat.
- Ibn Battuta was a great Muslim geographer.
- Muslim mathematicians invented algebra.
- Muslim doctors improved ancient medicine practices and changed how the sick were treated.
- Islamic art is generally in the style of geometric patterns and verses from the Quran.

Why Does It Matter?

The innovations of Muslim scholars expanded global trade and had an impact on future development.

photo: Library of Congress

The man on the left wears the traditional clothes of a Muslim scholar. Medieval Muslim scholars preserved and improved upon ancient philosophies, leaving a wealth of knowledge for Europe to explore during the Renaissance.

Name _____ Date _____

GRAPHIC ORGANIZER: GREASES Chart

Use this GREASES Chart to record details about life in Islamic society. For supporting resources, go to Empire, Belief, and Power > Origins of Islam and Early Islamic Empires > Life in the Islamic Empires > Explore > Geography and Trade.

	What I See	My Conclusions
Government		
Religion		
Economic		
Art & Architecture		
Science & Technology		
Environment		
Social & Cultural Values		

Name _____ **Date** _____

EXPLORE: FOCUS QUESTIONS

Using what you learned from the Core Interactive Text, answer each page's focus question:

Geography and Trade

How did the geography of the Arabian Peninsula affect how people in the region traded?

_____
_____
_____

The Spread of Islam

How did traders help to spread Islam?

_____
_____
_____

The Ottomans

How did Islam become the primary religion for powerful empires?

_____
_____
_____

Persia and South Asia

How did other Islamic empires expand their influence?

_____
_____
_____

Islamic Society

How did Islam affect society in the Muslim empires?

_____
_____
_____

Name _____ Date _____

EXPLORE: FOCUS QUESTIONS *(continued)*

The Role of Other Religions
How were members of other religions treated in the Islamic empires?

_____

_____

_____

Muslim Scholars
How did Muslim scholars use the past work of ancient civilizations?

_____

_____

_____

Advances in the Sciences and Mathematics
What advances were made by Muslim scholars?

_____

_____

_____

Medical Knowledge
What advances did Islamic society make in medicine?

_____

_____

_____

Islamic Art
How did the spread of Islam shape art and architecture?

_____

_____

_____

PROJECTS AND ASSESSMENTS

Explain Activities

ACTIVITY TYPE: DIAGRAM

Buddhism, Christianity, Islam, and Judaism

In this Diagram activity, you will use at least 10 words from the word bank to create a mind map that shows connections among the ideas in four religions: Buddhism, Christianity, Islam, and Judaism.

ACTIVITY TYPE: ENCYCLOPEDIA ENTRY

Life in the Islamic Empires

In this Encyclopedia Entry activity, you will create an entry for Abbas the Great, Ibn Battuta, or Muhammed Al-Khwarizmi.

ACTIVITY TYPE: SOCIAL STUDIES EXPLANATION

Life in the Islamic Empires

In this Social Studies Explanation activity, you will use a template to assemble evidence from the sources you have explored. Then, you will write an answer to the Essential Question and defend your answer with supporting evidence.

Elaborate Activities

photo: Discovery Education

INVESTIGATION TYPE: HISTORICAL PERSPECTIVES

Life in the Islamic Empires

In this Historical Perspectives Investigation, your mission is to get to know four individuals from the Islamic empires (550–1650) and explore the perspectives you think each would have on key issues of the day.

photo: Getty Images

ACTIVITY TYPE: ROLE PLAY

Life in the Islamic Empires

In this Role Play activity, you will take on the role of a European trader who has just done business with a Muslim trader for the first time after the end of the Crusades. You will write a journal entry about your interaction with that trader and explain how the experience has changed the way you think about the Muslims.

PROJECTS AND ASSESSMENTS *(continued)*

photo: Library of Congress

ACTIVITY TYPE: YOU AS ARTIST

The Arabian Nights

In this You as Artist activity, you will read and discuss a story from The Arabian Nights and then write a modern folktale based on the same theme.

photo: Getty Images

ACTIVITY TYPE: DOCUMENT-BASED INVESTIGATION

Life in the Islamic Empires

In this Document-Based Investigation, you will examine various sources and investigate this question: In what ways did other cultures impact the development of the Islamic empires?

Evaluate Activities

BRIEF-CONSTRUCTED RESPONSE (BCR)

Life in the Islamic Empires

EXTENDED-CONSTRUCTED RESPONSE (ECR)

Life in the Islamic Empires

UNIT 2: POWER AND CHANGE IN ASIA, AFRICA, AND THE AMERICAS

Chapter 5: South Asia and China

5.1 South Asia

LESSON OVERVIEW

Lesson Objectives:

By the end of this lesson, you should be able to:

- Describe the cultural, religious, and economic impact of the reunification of South Asia under the Gupta Empire.

- Analyze the changes in and growth of South Asian religions between 300 and 1200 CE.

- Describe the impact of Islam and the founding of the Delhi Sultanate on South Asia.

Key Vocabulary

Bhakti movement, Buddhism, Gupta Empire, Jainism, Mahayana Buddhism, pilgrimage, Sanskrit, Silk Road

Lesson Essential Question:

What changes and accomplishments defined India's Golden Age?

FLASHCARDS

1 India's Golden Age

The Gupta and Chola dynasties united India in peace and prosperity and created a rich culture that spread throughout South Asia.

- Chandra Gupta I took control of North India in 320. His son, Samudra, expanded the Gupta Empire until it reached from the Himalaya Mountains in the north, to the Indus Valley in the west, to Myanmar in the east.
- During the Gupta Empire, a Buddhist monk named Faxian made a pilgrimage from China to India to study and translate Buddhist texts.
- The Gupta age was one of peace and prosperity. Chandra II was a patron of the arts. Many discoveries were made, including the foundations of math and astronomy, the game of chess, and the crystallization of sugar.
- The Gupta Empire fell around 550 after a century of attacks from the Hunas of Central Asia, also called the Hepthalites or Huns.
- After the fall of the Guptas, the Chola dynasty rose to power in South India. Like the Guptas, the Cholas were patrons of the arts, especially architecture.

Why Does It Matter?

The cultural developments that emerged during the Gupta and Chola ages would have a strong influence on other parts of the world, including western Asia and Europe.

photo: Los Angeles County Museum of Art
This print of a bodhisattva, or Buddhist holy figure, was created in Nepal or Tibet during the 1800s.

2 The Religions of South Asia

Hinduism and Buddhism were the two main religions of medieval India. Islam became a third religion under the Delhi Sultanate.

- Both the Guptas and the Cholas were Hindu. The practice of Buddhism declined and in some cases went underground.
- During the medieval period, both Buddhism and Hinduism further developed their ascetic, or monastic, traditions.
- The bhakti tradition in Hinduism was open to anyone regardless of gender or caste. It gave rise to the ecstatic poetry and teachings of Ramananda and Mirabai.
- In 1206, Muslim armies from Central Asia captured North India and established the Delhi Sultanate.
- The Delhi Sultanate introduced Islam to North India and controlled northern South Asia for several centuries. Many South Asians converted to Islam, though Hinduism remained the most popular religion. Buddhism continued to decline, though it spread to East Asia.

Why Does It Matter?

Hinduism, Buddhism, and Islam made significant contributions to the culture of medieval India and South Asia.

photo: Library of Congress
Hindu and Buddhist practices have both similarities and differences.

FLASHCARDS *(continued)*

3 ### South Asia and the World

South Asian culture and religions spread to many parts of the world through pilgrimage and trade, by land and by sea.

- **Hinduism spread mainly to the south and east, into countries like Khmer, Indonesia, Cambodia, and Vietnam. Hinduism changed very little as new countries adopted it.**

- **Buddhism spread north, into countries such as Nepal, Tibet, Korea, China, and Japan. Buddhism changed more than Hinduism as it spread, producing the Mahayana and Zen forms.**

- **Pilgrims from China, like Fazian and Xuanzang, traveled to India and brought back translations of Buddhist texts.**

- **Scientific and mathematical discoveries were carried to Europe along with trade goods from India.**

- **Desire for more direct trade with India led to the European Age of Exploration.**

Why Does It Matter?

As the culture and discoveries of South Asia spread from India east into the rest of Asia and west into Europe, they helped shape the cultures, religions, and scientific discoveries of those regions. Many of the ideas that traveled to Europe inspired the European Renaissance, while desire for more direct trade with India led to the Age of Exploration and the European colonization of large parts of the world, including North and South America.

photo: Pixabay

This bronze Buddha statue in Japan was cast in 1252.

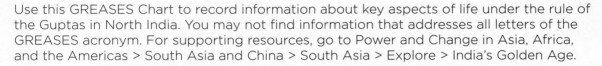

Name _____ **Date** _____

GRAPHIC ORGANIZER: GREASES Chart

Use this GREASES Chart to record information about key aspects of life under the rule of the Guptas in North India. You may not find information that addresses all letters of the GREASES acronym. For supporting resources, go to Power and Change in Asia, Africa, and the Americas > South Asia and China > South Asia > Explore > India's Golden Age.

	What I See	My Conclusions
Government		
Religion		
Economic		
Art & Architecture		
Science & Technology		
Environment		
Social & Cultural Values		

Name _____ **Date** _____

GRAPHIC ORGANIZER: Comparison Chart

Use this Comparison Chart to summarize and record details about Hinduism and Buddhism in India between 300 and 1200 CE. For supporting resources, go to Power and Change in Asia, Africa, and the Americas > South Asia and China > South Asia > Explore > India After the Guptas.

Religion	Who Is/Are the Main God/Gods or Spiritual Figures?	What Are the Key Beliefs?	What Are the Important Works of Literature or Sacred Texts?
Hinduism			
Buddhism			

Name _____ **Date** _____

GRAPHIC ORGANIZER: Change Over Time Chart

Use this Change Over Time Chart to record how Buddhism changed between 300 and 1200 CE. For supporting resources, go to Power and Change in Asia, Africa, and the Americas > South Asia and China > South Asia > Explore > Love Poems to God.

Before:

After:

Changes:

Name _____ Date _____

EXPLORE: FOCUS QUESTIONS

Using what you learned from the Core Interactive Text, answer each page's focus question:

Rise of the Gupta Empire

In what ways did the Gupta Empire consolidate power and culture in South Asia?

_____
_____
_____

India's Golden Age

What were the most important scientific and cultural contributions of the Gupta Empire?

_____
_____
_____

India After the Guptas

How did South Asia change after the Gupta era?

_____
_____
_____

Religious Awakenings

What impact did the bhakti movement have on the culture of medieval South Asia?

_____
_____
_____

Love Poems to God

Who were Ramananda and Mirabai?

_____
_____
_____

Name _____   Date _____

EXPLORE: FOCUS QUESTIONS *(continued)*

The Growth of Faiths
How did Hinduism and Buddhism spread and change?

_____

_____

_____

East Meets West
How did South Asia influence medieval Europe?

_____

_____

_____

PROJECTS AND ASSESSMENTS

Explain Activities

ACTIVITY TYPE: ADVERTISEMENT

A New Delight!

In this activity, you will create an advertisement for a new discovery or innovation from medieval South Asia.

ACTIVITY TYPE: QUICK WRITE

Seeking the Spiritual

In this activity, you will write a paragraph explaining how practicing Buddhism and Hinduism became easier and more accessible in medieval South Asia under Gupta and Chola rule.

ACTIVITY TYPE: SOCIAL STUDIES EXPLANATION

South Asia

In this Social Studies Explanation activity, you will use a template to assemble evidence from the sources you have explored. Then, you will write an answer to the Essential Question and defend your answer with supporting evidence.

Elaborate Activities

photo: Paul Fuqua

ACTIVITY TYPE: CURRENT EVENTS CONNECTION

Indian Innovations – Then and Now

In this activity, you will research one of the innovations that came out of medieval India. You will choose cotton, base-10 numbers, or spices. Then, you will explain how your chosen innovation changed the world of medieval South Asia and how it helped create our modern world.

PROJECTS AND ASSESSMENTS *(continued)*

photo: Getty Images

ACTIVITY TYPE: SAY WHAT?

The Journals of Xuanzang

In this activity, you will "translate" a passage from the journals of the Chinese Buddhist monk Xuanzang and analyze what the text tells us about the culture and people of medieval India.

Evaluate Activities

BRIEF-CONSTRUCTED RESPONSE (BCR)

India's Golden Age

EXTENDED-CONSTRUCTED RESPONSE (ECR)

The Songs of Mirabai

UNIT 2: POWER AND CHANGE IN ASIA, AFRICA, AND THE AMERICAS

Chapter 5: South Asia and China

5.2 China's Reunification and Development

photo: IRC

LESSON OVERVIEW

Lesson Objectives:

By the end of this lesson, you should be able to:

- **Explain the reasons for the fracturing of China.**
- **Identify important Chinese dynasties (Tang dynasty, Song dynasty) and the developments of Chinese culture during this era before the Mongol invasion.**
- **Analyze the evolution of Confucianism during this period and its impact on governmental systems.**

Key Vocabulary

Buddhism, census, Chang'an, China, civil war, Confucianism, Daoism / Taoism, Europe, Grand School, Great Wall of China, Han dynasty, junk, Li Yuan, Mandate of Heaven, Marco Polo, Mediterranean Sea, Middle East, Neo-Confucianism, Silk Road, Song dynasty, Tang Empire, unification, Yellow Turban Rebellion

Lesson Essential Question:

What were the greatest achievements of the Tang and Song dynasties?

FLASHCARDS

1 Fall of the Han Dynasty and the Three Kingdoms Period

The lack of a strong emperor allowed internal fighting to weaken the central government, making it vulnerable.

- The weakness of Emperor Xian allowed greedy court officials to seize power for themselves.
- Power struggles between the officials, clans of the empress, and court servants further weakened China.
- The ideals of Daoism spread throughout the Chinese peasants, inspiring them to revolt.
- Powerful warlords seized control and divided China into the Three Kingdoms.
- The Wei and Jin dynasties attempted to reunify China, but both failed.

Why Does It Matter?

The events that caused the Han dynasty to fall continued to plague China until its reunification. The problems that the divided empire faced needed to be solved before China could reunify and flourish.

photo: Los Angeles County Museum of Art (www.lacma.org)
This bronze crossbow would have been a common and powerful weapon in the late Han dynasty.

2 A New Era of Imperial China

China was reunified under the Sui and Tang dynasties. The achievements of that era were carried into the Song dynasty.

- Many of the achievements of the short-lived Sui dynasty were continued by Li Yuan, founder of the Tang dynasty.
- Painting, ceramic sculpture, and literature reached a golden age in the Tang and Song dynasties.
- The Grand Canal made trade and travel easier within China.
- The Silk Road, which allowed trade with the West, reached its peak during the Tang dynasty.

Why Does It Matter?

A strong government and a united country allowed art and literature to flourish. Trade with the Western world brought great wealth and new ideas to China, enriching its culture. It also allowed Chinese ideas and influence to enter the West.

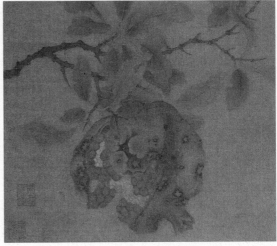

photo: Los Angeles County Museum of Art (www.lacma.org)
This painting on silk is one example of the development of Chinese art during the Song dynasty.

FLASHCARDS *(continued)*

3 **The Return of Confucianism**

Confucianism was restored to official government use during the Sui, Tang, and Song dynasties.

- Neo-Confucianism included elements from Daoism and Buddhism.
- Confucianism, which had been a minor philosophy, rose in popularity and importance.
- The Song dynasty used Neo-Confucianism to justify and strengthen its rule.
- Neo-Confucianism became the basis for a new meritocracy in the Song government.

Why Does It Matter?

During the Song dynasty, Neo-Confucianism grew in popularity. Neo-Confucianism helped to strengthen and organize the government. A strong government in China helped to encourage the economic and cultural growth that occurred during the Song dynasty.

photo: Pixabay

The teachings of Confucius became popular again during the Song dynasty.

Name _____ **Date** _____

GRAPHIC ORGANIZER: Change Over Time Chart

Use this Change Over Time Chart to list factors that contributed to the fall of the Han dynasty, the different dynasties that took power, and their characteristics. For supporting resources, go to Power and Change in Asia, Africa, and the Americas > South Asia and China > China's Reunification and Development > Explore > The Fall of the Han Dynasty.

Before:	After:

Changes:

Name _____ **Date** _____

 GRAPHIC ORGANIZER: Comparison Chart

Use this Comparison Chart to record the different dynasties that took power and their characteristics. For supporting resources, go to Power and Change in Asia, Africa, and the Americas > South Asia and China > China's Reunification and Development > Explore > The Tang Dynasty.

Tang Dynasty	Song Dynasty
How Did It Come to Power?	How Did It Come to Power?
Important Leader(s) and Why They Were Important:	Important Leader(s) and Why They Were Important:

Name _____ **Date** _____

GRAPHIC ORGANIZER: Comparison Chart *(continued)*

Tang Dynasty	Song Dynasty
New Inventions and/or Products:	New Inventions and/or Products:
Trends in the Arts:	Trends in the Arts:
Important Artist(s):	Important Artist(s):

Name _____ **Date** _____

GRAPHIC ORGANIZER: Comparison Chart *(continued)*

Similarities Between the Tang and Song Dynasties
Ways They Came to Power:
Leaders:
New Inventions or Products:
Arts and Artists:

Name _____ Date _____

GRAPHIC ORGANIZER: Comparison Chart *(continued)*

Differences Between the Tang and Song Dynasties
Ways They Came to Power:
Leaders:
New Inventions or Products:
Arts and Artists:

Name _____ **Date** _____

GRAPHIC ORGANIZER: Comparison Chart *(continued)*

Impact of Reunificaiton

Name _____ **Date** _____

EXPLORE: FOCUS QUESTIONS

Using what you learned from the Core Interactive Text, answer each page's focus question:

The Fall of the Han Dynasty
What led to the collapse of the Han dynasty?

_____

_____

_____

The Three Kingdoms
What happened after the fall of the Han dynasty?

_____

_____

_____

The Sui Dynasty
How was China finally reunited?

_____

_____

_____

The Tang Dynasty
How did the Tang dynasty succeed where the Sui dynasty failed?

_____

_____

_____

A Golden Age
How did the Song dynasty rise to power?

_____

_____

_____

Name _____ **Date** _____

EXPLORE: FOCUS QUESTIONS *(continued)*

Art and War
What achievements occurred during the Song dynasty?

_____
_____
_____

Silk and the Silk Road
How did silk impact trade in China?

_____
_____
_____

The Rise of Neo-Confucianism
How did Confucianism rise in popularity during the Song dynasty?

_____
_____
_____

Neo-Confucianism in the Song Dynasty
Why was Neo-Confucianism important to the Song dynasty?

_____
_____
_____

PROJECTS AND ASSESSMENTS

Explain Activities

ACTIVITY TYPE: VISUALIZATION

Reunifying China

In this Visualization activity, you will create a slideshow presenting the six most important changes or events occurring between the fall of the Han dynasty and the rise of the Song dynasty.

ACTIVITY TYPE: QUICK WRITE

Traveling the Silk Road

In this Quick Write, you will take the role of a Tang or Song dynasty merchant and write a fictional journal entry about preparing for a journey along the Silk Road.

ACTIVITY TYPE: SOCIAL STUDIES EXPLANATION

China's Reunification and Development

In this Social Studies Explanation activity, you will use a template to assemble evidence from the sources you have explored. Then, you will write an answer to the Essential Question and defend your answer with supporting evidence.

Elaborate Activities

photo: Getty Images

INVESTIGATION TYPE: TIMELINE INQUIRY

The Reunification of China

How did China move from war and chaos to a "Golden Age" under the Tang dynasty? In this activity, you will use the interactive Timeline Inquiry tool to learn about the changes that occurred in China from 220 to 1279.

photo: Paul Fuqua

ACTIVITY TYPE: PITCH YOUR IDEA

Solving Problems with Technology

In this activity, you will invent a product that solves an everyday problem of the people of the Song empire. You will then propose your idea for a new invention to the Song emperor.

PROJECTS AND ASSESSMENTS *(continued)*

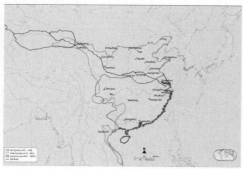

photo: Discovery Education

ACTIVITY TYPE: EXPRESS YOUR OPINION

Song and Tang Museum Exhibit

In this activity, you will research and evaluate some of the achievements of this period and present your findings in a museum exhibit.

photo: Getty Images

ACTIVITY TYPE: DOCUMENT-BASED INVESTIGATION

Chinese Reunification and Development

In this Document-Based Investigation, you will analyze source materials and investigate this question: How did the Chinese view merchants during the Tang and Song dynasties?

Evaluate Activities

BRIEF-CONSTRUCTED RESPONSE (BCR)

China's Reunification and Development

EXTENDED-CONSTRUCTED RESPONSE (ECR)

China's Reunification and Development

UNIT 2: POWER AND CHANGE IN ASIA, AFRICA, AND THE AMERICAS

Chapter 5: South Asia and China

5.3 The Mongols

photo: Getty Images

LESSON OVERVIEW

Lesson Objectives:

By the end of this lesson, you should be able to:

- **Explain the expansion of the Mongolian Empire.**
- **Analyze the impact of Mongol rule on Chinese civilization and other cultures.**

Lesson Essential Question:

How did Mongol conquest change relations between regional societies?

Key Vocabulary

Africa, Baghdad, Beijing, Black Sea, Catholic Church, China, Christopher Columbus, commonwealth, Crusaders / Crusades, England, Eurasia, Genghis Khan, Gobi Desert, Great Schism, Great Wall of China, Himalayas, Huns, Iraq, John Calvin, King Henry VIII, Korea, Marco Polo, Martin Luther, Mediterranean Sea, Mongolia, Mongols, Muslims, New Testament, nomadic, Pax Mongolica, Pax Romana, Persian Gulf, pope, Protestant Church, Protestant Reformation, Protestantism, reform / social reform, Silk Road, Song dynasty, steppe, trade, William Tyndale

FLASHCARDS

1 The Mongols in War

Under Genghis Khan and his successors, the Mongols conquered the largest empire in history up to that time.

- Genghis Khan united the warring tribes of the steppe and began to invade neighboring regions.
- The Mongols used swift attacks and terrifying tactics to demoralize their enemies and conquer their territory.
- At its largest, the Mongolian Empire was bordered by the Pacific Ocean, the Himalaya Mountains, the Black Sea, and the Persian Gulf.

Why Does It Matter?

In just 50 years, a small nomadic tribe united many nations and cultural groups under its rule.

SHOOTING AT PURSUERS.

photo: Abbot, Jacob. Genghis Khan. New York, NY: Harper & Brothers Publishers, 1901.

The mounted warriors of the Mongol Empire provided a distinct advantage and helped them to conquer a vast amount of land.

2 The Mongols at Peace

After their conquests, the Mongols promoted trade and cultural exchange throughout their empire and beyond.

- The Mongols did not impose their language and culture on the peoples they conquered.
- The power of the Mongol Empire led to a period of stability that allowed business and trade to grow.
- Mongols controlled the trade routes and encouraged the exchange of goods and ideas among various cultural regions of their empire.
- Marco Polo visited China from Europe and was a guest of Kublai Khan and an official of his government.
- Marco Polo's description of China increased the demand for Chinese goods in Europe.

Why Does It Matter?

Mongol rulers, especially Kublai Khan, increased the trade in goods and cultural ideas beyond the borders of their empire.

oto: Pixabay

While the Mongols were masters of horsemanship, this animal was most frequently used by traders to carry goods across their empire. Why do you think this was so?

Name _____ Date _____

GRAPHIC ORGANIZER: GREASES Chart

Use this GREASES Chart to take notes on the Mongol Empire. For supporting resources, go to Power and Change in Asia, Africa, and the Americas > South Asia and China > The Mongols > Explore > The Beginnings of the Mongol Empire.

Government	
Religion	
Economic	
Art & Architecture	
Science & Technology	
Environment	
Social & Cultural Values	

Name _____ **Date** _____

GRAPHIC ORGANIZER: Summary Frames

Use these Summary Frames to illustrate important details in the expansion of the Mongol Empire from 1215 to 1290. For supporting resources, go to Power and Change in Asia, Africa, and the Americas > South Asia and China > The Mongols > Explore > From China to Hungary.

_____ _____ _____

_____ _____ _____

_____ _____ _____

_____ _____ _____

Name _____ **Date** _____

GRAPHIC ORGANIZER: Summary Frames *(continued)*

_____   _____   _____

_____   _____   _____

_____   _____   _____

Name _____ Date _____

EXPLORE: FOCUS QUESTIONS

Using what you learned from the Core Interactive Text, answer each page's focus question:

The Beginnings of the Mongol Empire

How did Genghis Khan establish the Mongol Empire?

_____
_____
_____

Laws of the Mongol Empire

How did Genghis Khan rule his empire?

_____
_____
_____

The Mongol Conquest of China

How did the Mongols gain control of China?

_____
_____
_____

Mongol Conquests

How did the Mongols expand their empire in Asia?

_____
_____
_____

From China to Hungary

What happened to the Mongol Empire after Genghis Khan died?

_____
_____
_____

Name _____ **Date** _____

EXPLORE: FOCUS QUESTIONS *(continued)*

Life Under the Mongols
What was life like in the Mongol Empire?

_____

_____

_____

The Pax Mongolica
How did trade flourish under the Mongols?

_____

_____

_____

West Meets East
Who was Marco Polo?

_____

_____

_____

Marco Polo's Book
How did Marco Polo's travels influence Europe?

_____

_____

_____

PROJECTS AND ASSESSMENTS

Explain Activities

ACTIVITY TYPE: DIAGRAM

The Mongols

Use at least eight words from the Word Bank to create a graphic response to the Essential Question. On a separate sheet of paper, summarize your map by describing how the map shows how the Mongol conquest changed relations between societies.

ACTIVITY TYPE: YOU AS JOURNALIST

The Mongols

In this activity, you will imagine you are a reporter in the 1200s, interviewing a survivor of a recent attack by Mongol warriors. In the space provided, write the transcript of an interview between you and the survivor.

ACTIVITY TYPE: SOCIAL STUDIES EXPLANATION

The Mongols

In this Social Studies Explanation activity, you will use a template to assemble evidence from the sources you have explored. Then, you will write an answer to the Essential Question and defend your answer with supporting evidence.

Elaborate Activities

photo: Getty Images

INVESTIGATION TYPE: TIMELINE MAP

The Mongol Empire

What political and cultural changes enabled the Mongols to conquer such a large empire in such a short period of time? Your mission is to determine how the Mongols grew from a small group of battling tribes into one of the largest empires in history.

photo: Getty Images

ACTIVITY TYPE: STUDENT SLEUTH

Mongols—Savage or Misunderstood?

In this activity, you will analyze a 19th-century illustration of Genghis Khan and his warriors. Then, you will read a few firsthand descriptions of the Mongolians from 13th-century chroniclers. Finally, you will write a newspaper article in which you report the facts about the Mongolians.

PROJECTS AND ASSESSMENTS *(continued)*

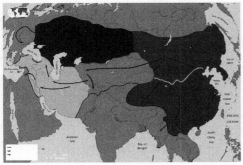

photo: Discovery Education

ACTIVITY TYPE: CURRENT EVENTS CONNECTION

Pax Mongolica and Pax Romana

In this activity, you will create a presentation about how the Pax Mongolica compares to the Pax Romana. You will then create a slideshow to use as a visual aid in your presentation to illustrate how these concepts were alike and different in terms of their impact on their respective societies.

photo: Getty Images

ACTIVITY TYPE: DOCUMENT-BASED INVESTIGATION

The Mongols

In this Document-Based Investigation, you will analyze source materials and investigate this question: How did the Mongol Empire influence cultures in Europe, Central Asia, and East Asia? Did it cause greater cultural destruction or greater cultural exchange?

Evaluate Activities

BRIEF-CONSTRUCTED RESPONSE (BCR)

The Mongolians

EXTENDED-CONSTRUCTED RESPONSE (ECR)

The Mongolians

UNIT 2: POWER AND CHANGE IN ASIA, AFRICA, AND THE AMERICAS

Chapter 5: South Asia and China

5.4 The Ming Dynasty

LESSON OVERVIEW

Lesson Objectives:

By the end of this lesson, you should be able to:

- Explain how trade under the Ming dynasty spread Chinese ideas and goods across the world.
- Discuss how the expansion of trade in China led to the growth of the empire and its people.
- Evaluate the decision by Ming emperors to cut off overseas expeditions and outlaw foreign trade.

Key Vocabulary

Africa, Asia, Beijing, Europe, Genghis Khan, Great Wall of China, gunpowder, India, Indian Ocean, junk, Ming dynasty, Mongols, porcelain, Silk Road, Song dynasty, Zheng He, Zhu Yuanzhang

Lesson Essential Question:

How did trade shape Chinese society during the Ming dynasty?

FLASHCARDS

1 Chinese Ideas Spread

After the Ming dynasty took control of China from the Mongols, Chinese ideas and goods spread across the world.

- Admiral Zheng He's ocean journeys increased China's trade and status.
- The Chinese continued to use and improve on navigational tools and ship design, which helped improve trade and lead to exploration.
- During the Ming dynasty, the Chinese improved the process of papermaking and continued to use moveable type, which made the manufacture of books much quicker.
- Porcelain and silk were highly valued Chinese exports.

Why Does It Matter?

Chinese advances in arts and science improved their quality of life and enhanced their status among other nations.

photo: Pixabay

A Chinese nobleman on horseback wears silk, highly sought after by the rest of the world during this time period.

2 As Trade Expands, the Empire Grows

The expansion of trade led to the growth of the Ming dynasty's empire and its people.

- Porcelain, jade, silk, and other goods reached the West by the Silk Road.
- The growth in trade led to a higher standard of living for Chinese merchants.
- The stability of the Ming Empire allowed art, poetry, and literature to thrive.

Why Does It Matter?

As trade grew, the Chinese merchant class became more powerful. This relatively peaceful and prosperous time in China's history also allowed them to pursue artistic endeavors such as art, poetry, and literature.

photo: Pixabay

Blue and white porcelain Ming vases are still popular today.

FLASHCARDS *(continued)*

3 Overseas Trade Ends

China produced several goods other nations were eager to import. But in 1433, the Ming emperor cut off trade and outlawed overseas expeditions.

- **The Ming government banned the construction of large ships.**
- **Traders were forced to come to China to obtain Chinese goods.**
- **Explorers sought new trade routes to the East.**

Why Does It Matter?

At the height of its commercial activity, Chinese leaders decided to reduce their contact with the rest of the world. This motivated European explorers to find new routes to the East and indirectly led to the European discovery of America.

photo: From The New York Public Library

The Chinese junk was such a successful design that it is still in use today. In 1433, the Chinese government halted the construction of large ships, forcing explorers to find new ways to reach China.

Name _____ Date _____

GRAPHIC ORGANIZER: GREASES Chart

Use this GREASES Chart to describe the Ming dynasty. For supporting resources, go to Power and Change in Asia, Africa, and the Americas > South Asia and China > The Ming Dynasty > Explore > Birth of a Dynasty.

Government	
Religion	
Economic	
Art & **A**rchitecture	
Science & **T**echnology	
Environment	
Social & **C**ultural Values	

Name _____ **Date** _____

GRAPHIC ORGANIZER: Summary Frames

Use these Summary Frames to analyze the importance of trade to China and the impact of China closing its borders. For supporting resources, go to Power and Change in Asia, Africa, and the Americas > South Asia and China > The Ming Dynasty > Explore > Transcontinental Trade.

Positive Aspects of Foreign Trade

_____   _____   _____

_____   _____   _____

_____   _____   _____

Negative Aspects of Foreign Trade

_____   _____   _____

_____   _____   _____

_____   _____   _____

© Discovery Education | www.DiscoveryEducation.com

Name _____ Date _____

EXPLORE: FOCUS QUESTIONS

Using what you learned from the Core Interactive Text, answer each page's focus question:

Birth of a Dynasty
How did the Ming dynasty begin?

_____

_____

_____

Culture and Trade
How did a renewed interest in culture increase trade during the Ming dynasty?

_____

_____

_____

Masters of the Oceans
How did the Ming rule the seas?

_____

_____

_____

The Explorations of Admiral Zheng He
How did advances in navigation and shipbuilding impact exploration?

_____

_____

_____

Reading and Writing
How did culture grow during the Ming dynasty?

_____

_____

_____

Name _____ **Date** _____

EXPLORE: FOCUS QUESTIONS *(continued)*

Transcontinental Trade
How did demand for Chinese products abroad impact trade?

_____
_____
_____

The Empire Turns Inward
Why did Ming emperors cut off outside trade and ban overseas expeditions?

_____
_____
_____

PROJECTS AND ASSESSMENTS

Explain Activities

ACTIVITY TYPE: VISUALIZATION

The Ming Dynasty

Use your Summary Frames graphic organizer, Categorization Chart graphic organizer, and the information gathered from the concept to create a comic book or series of cartoons that illustrate the adventures and events in the life of Admiral Zheng He during the Ming dynasty.

ACTIVITY TYPE: QUICK WRITE

The Ming Dynasty

In this Quick Write, you will take the perspective of a person during the Ming dynasty and write a description of your life at the time.

ACTIVITY TYPE: SOCIAL STUDIES EXPLANATION

The Ming Dynasty

In this Social Studies Explanation activity, you will use a template to assemble evidence from the sources you have explored. Then, you will write an answer to the Essential Question and defend your answer with supporting evidence.

Elaborate Activities

photo: Discovery Education

INVESTIGATION TYPE: HISTORICAL PERSPECTIVES

Ming Dynasty

Your mission is to read the profiles of four individuals who lived during the Ming dynasty and explore the perspective each might have on key issues of the day.

photo: Pixabay

ACTIVITY TYPE: CURRENT EVENTS CONNECTION

China's Trade Policies

In this activity, you will prepare a written essay or a speech that compares and contrasts the trade policies during the Ming dynasty with trade policies today and explain the effects on Chinese society of each set of policies.

PROJECTS AND ASSESSMENTS *(continued)*

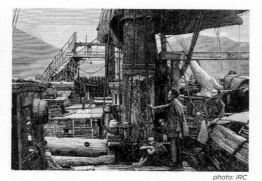

photo: IRC

ACTIVITY TYPE: PITCH YOUR IDEA

Ming Trade Policies

In this activity, you will create a presentation that suggests one of two things: that the sea trade should be resumed or that the ban on sea trade should be continued. The presentation should be persuasive enough to convince the emperor of your position.

photo: Getty Images

ACTIVITY TYPE: DOCUMENT-BASED INVESTIGATION

The Ming Dynasty

In this Document-Based Investigation, you will analyze source materials and investigate this question: Was China isolated during the Ming dynasty?

photo: Los Angeles County Museum of Art (www.lacma.org)

ACTIVITY TYPE: DOCUMENT-BASED INVESTIGATION

Trade and Innovation in Ming China

In this activity, you will draft the opening statement for a public debate or create a newspaper article for the opening of an exhibit in a museum. Your statement or article will answer this question: Did trade or innovations have a greater influence on life in China during the Ming dynasty?

Evaluate Activities

BRIEF-CONSTRUCTED RESPONSE (BCR)

Ming Sailors

EXTENDED-CONSTRUCTED RESPONSE (ECR)

Trade in the Ming Dynasty

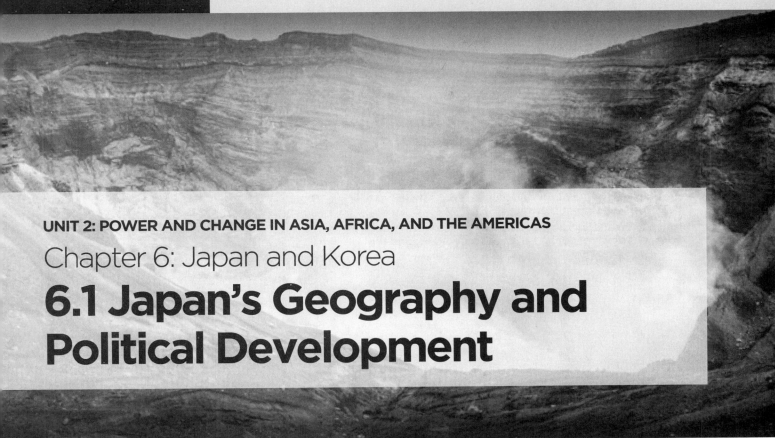

photo: IRC

UNIT 2: POWER AND CHANGE IN ASIA, AFRICA, AND THE AMERICAS

Chapter 6: Japan and Korea

6.1 Japan's Geography and Political Development

LESSON OVERVIEW

Lesson Objectives:

By the end of this lesson, you should be able to:

- Locate Japan's boundaries, important cities, and bodies of water on a map.

- Describe how the geography of the region shaped the way of life of the people living there.

- Trace the major political, economic, and religious developments in Japanese history.

Lesson Essential Question:

How did physical geography influence Japan's cultural development?

Key Vocabulary

Ainu, archipelago, Asia, Buddhism, China, Confucius, daimyo, Edo, empire, Heian period, Japan, Kyoto, Lady Murasaki, Minamoto Yoritomo, Mount Fuji, Prince Shotoku, province, shogun, The Tale of Genji, The Tale of the Heike, Tokugawa Ieyasu, Tokugawa shogunate, Tokyo, Toyotomi Hideyoshi

FLASHCARDS

1 Japan in the World

Japan's nearness to, and separation from, the Asian mainland was one of the key factors in its history.

- Japan is an archipelago of islands off the eastern coast of Asia.
- Japan was created by shifting tectonic plates. These plates are still active today and are responsible for the earthquakes that commonly occur in Japan. The climate also produces violent storms.
- Tokyo is the nation's capital and one of the world's largest cities, but much of Japan's history centered around the earlier capital of Kyoto.

Why Does It Matter?

Like other island nations, such as Britain, the sea protected Japan from outside influence during much of its history and helped produce its culture.

photo: Pixabay

Japan is a land of great natural beauty. Earthquakes, volcanoes, and violent storms have helped shape Japan's natural environment and the culture of its people.

2 Watery Land, Mountainous Land

Japan's isolation led it to develop a unique culture, but it also absorbed important elements from Chinese culture.

- The mountains running through the islands of Japan made sea travel easier than land travel.
- The ocean isolated Japan from the cultures of nearby mainland countries.
- Because it was easy to produce in Japan's climate, rice became an important crop in Japan.

Why Does It Matter?

The difficulty of land travel made it hard for any one ruler to dominate all of Japan. Being surrounded by ocean made it difficult for any land-based power to invade Japan.

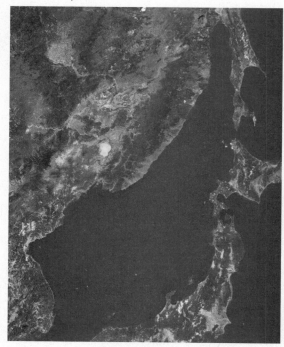

photo: Getty Images

This satellite image shows the location of the Japanese archipelago in relation to mainland Asia and its mountainous terrain.

FLASHCARDS

3 ▸ Emperor, Shogun, and Daimyo

Japan's written history began with contact with China and includes several periods characterized by political, cultural, and religious movements.

- During the Heian period (794–1185), emperors ruled Japan, but the government was dominated by a noble family that intermarried with the emperors.
- Prince Shotoku embraced Chinese culture and encouraged the Japanese to learn from the Chinese.
- During the Heian period, Japan absorbed many elements of Chinese culture.
- Among these elements were Buddhism, ideas of government, the Chinese writing system, and the arts.
- Feudal warfare between daimyo and their samurai armies brought about the end of the Heian culture, and Minamoto Toyotomi became the first shogun.
- In 1543, Portuguese ships reached Japan, beginning several decades of contact between Japan and Europe that were to influence Japanese warfare and politics.
- Three powerful rulers unified Japan at the end of the 1500s and in the early 1600s. Tokugawa Ieyasu became shogun in 1603, and the Tokugawa Shogunate isolated Japan from the rest of the world.

Why Does It Matter?

Geography, power, politics, religion, and economics combined to shape the course of Japanese history.

photo: Los Angeles County Museum of Art (www.lacma.org)
Ieyasu established the Tokugawa Shogunate, which closed Japan to the outside world and ruled for more than two centuries.

Name _____ **Date** _____

 GRAPHIC ORGANIZER: Comparison Chart

Use this Comparison Chart to list the major geographical features of Japan and how they affected its people and culture. For supporting resources, go to Power and Change in Asia, Africa, and the Americas > Japan and Korea > Japan's Geography and Political Development > Explore > An Island Nation.

	Positive	Negative
Geograpical Feature		
Your Prediction		
Effect on Society		

© Discovery Education | www.DiscoveryEducation.com

Name _____ **Date** _____

GRAPHIC ORGANIZER: Change Over Time Chart

Use this Change Over Time Chart to compare Japan's political structure before and after the introduction of Buddhist and Chinese influences. For supporting resources, go to Power and Change in Asia, Africa, and the Americas > Japan and Korea > Japan's Geography and Political Development > Explore > A Divine Emperor.

Before:	After:

Changes:

Name _____ Date _____

GRAPHIC ORGANIZER: Summary Frames

Use these Summary Frames to highlight the important aspects of political and cultural life at the Heian court. For supporting resources, go to Power and Change in Asia, Africa, and the Americas > Japan and Korea > Japan's Geography and Political Development > Explore > Politics in the Heian Court.

© Discovery Education | www.DiscoveryEducation.com

Name _____ Date _____

GRAPHIC ORGANIZER: Summary Frames *(continued)*

Name _____ **Date** _____

GRAPHIC ORGANIZER: Summary Frames *(continued)*

_____   _____   _____

_____   _____   _____

_____   _____   _____

_____   _____   _____

_____   _____   _____

_____   _____   _____

Name _____ **Date** _____

EXPLORE: FOCUS QUESTIONS

Using what you learned from the Core Interactive Text, answer each page's focus question:

An Island Nation

What are the important geographical features of Japan?

_____

_____

_____

Potential Threats

What problems are caused by Japan's location?

_____

_____

_____

An Island People

How have mountains and sea affected the Japanese people?

_____

_____

_____

A Divine Emperor

Who ruled early Japan?

_____

_____

_____

A Practical Prince

Who was Prince Shotoku?

_____

_____

Name _____ Date _____

EXPLORE: FOCUS QUESTIONS *(continued)*

Politics in the Heian Court
What was political life like at the Heian court?

_____
_____
_____
_____

At the Emperor's Court
What was cultural life like at the Heian court?

_____
_____
_____

The Rise of the Samurai
What events brought about the end of the Heian culture?

_____
_____
_____

Under the Shoguns
How did the samurai influence Japanese culture?

_____
_____
_____

The Three Unifiers
How was Japan unified?

_____
_____
_____

Turning Inward
Why did Japan close itself off to the outside world?

_____
_____
_____

PROJECTS AND ASSESSMENTS

Explain Activities

ACTIVITY TYPE: VISUALIZATION

Geography of Japan

In this activity, think about examples of geographical features that influenced Japan's history and culture. Collect pictures that represent these examples and paste them in the blank frames.

ACTIVITY TYPE: SOCIAL STUDIES EXPLANATION

Japan's Geography and Political Development

In this Social Studies Explanation activity, you will use a template to assemble evidence from the sources you have explored. Then, you will write an answer to the Essential Question and defend your answer with supporting evidence.

Elaborate Activities

photo: Gettty Images

INVESTIGATION TYPE: MAP-GUIDED INQUIRY

Geography and Political Development of Japan

How did physical geography influence Japan's cultural development? In this investigation, you will use the Map-Guided Inquiry interactive tool to examine how historic Japan compares to modern Japan on a map.

photo: Pixabay

ACTIVITY TYPE: STUDENT SLEUTH

Does Geography Make a Nation?

In this activity, you will analyze an excerpt from Hail's 1898 book, "Japan and Its Rescue." You will compare his observations about Japan to other examples and images of the country's geography and culture and then write a memo to your editor in which you comment on the accuracy of Hail's account and make a recommendation about whether to include the source.

PROJECTS AND ASSESSMENTS *(continued)*

photo: Los Angeles County Museum of Art (www.lacma.org)

ACTIVITY TYPE: SAY WHAT?

Life in the Heian Court

In this activity, you will read an excerpt from The Tale of Genji and translate it for modern times. Then, you will write a letter to Lady Murasaki, describing what her text taught you about life in the Heian court.

photo: Getty Images

ACTIVITY TYPE: DOCUMENT-BASED INVESTIGATION

Geography and Political Development of Japan

In this Document-Based Investigation, you will analyze source materials and investigate the following question: How did the shoguns of Japan gain and consolidate power?

photo: Pixabay

ACTIVITY TYPE: DOCUMENT-BASED INVESTIGATION

Geography and Religion

In this activity, you will write a speech explaining how geography has shaped the Japanese belief systems and whether you believe geography has had a greater influence on one belief system than the other. You will analyze resources about the two major religions, Shintoism and Buddhism.

Evaluate Activities

BRIEF-CONSTRUCTED RESPONSE (BCR)

Japan's Geography and Political Development

EXTENDED-CONSTRUCTED RESPONSE (ECR)

Japan's Geography and Political Development

UNIT 2: POWER AND CHANGE IN ASIA, AFRICA, AND THE AMERICAS

Chapter 6: Japan and Korea

6.2 Japanese Society

LESSON OVERVIEW

Lesson Objectives:

By the end of this lesson, you should be able to:

- Analyze the relationship between feudal power, military rank, and social status in shogunate Japan.
- Understand the connection between Zen Buddhism and Bushido.
- Identify important achievements and contributions of the Japanese people.

Key Vocabulary

artisan, Basho, Buddhism, Bushidŏ, civil war, daimyo, Edo, emperor, feudalism, haiku, Hokusai, Japan, merchant, Minamoto Yoritomo, peasant, Prince Shotoku, shogun, Tokugawa Ieyasu, Tokugawa shogunate, Toyotomi Hideyoshi, Zen Buddhism

Lesson Essential Question:

What effects did power and social class have on Japanese feudal society?

FLASHCARDS

1 Under the Shogun

Japan was unified but strictly regimented under the Tokugawa shogunate.

- The emperor was considered to be descended from the gods but had no political power.
- The shogun, or supreme military dictator, was the real ruler of the country.
- Large landowners, or daimyo, controlled local populations through samurai warriors who were loyal to them.
- Samurai were expected to set an example for the populace by following the code of Bushidŏ.
- Peasants made up the majority of the population and worked the land for the daimyo.
- Merchants and shopkeepers had low status but gained power through their control of trade and banking.
- The shogun maintained control over the daimyo by requiring them and their families to live in the capital every other year.

Why Does It Matter?

Under Japan's Tokugawa shogunate, social status was hereditary and closely tied to military rank or way of earning a living. Members of one social class could not move up to another social class. Individuals' social class affected all aspects of their lives.

photo: Library of Congress

How is this samurai dressed? Do you think this is what samurai wore when they went into battle?

2 Some Japanese Cultural Treasures

Under the Tokugawa shogunate, several aspects of Japanese culture evolved and flourished.

- Zen, a Japanese form of Buddhism, was the preferred religion of the samurai class.
- Woodblock printmaking developed as an art form and captured the lively urban culture of the merchant class.
- Haiku, a traditional Japanese form of poetry, gained its greatest expression in the years of the Tokugawa shogunate.

Why Does It Matter?

The era of the shoguns and the samurai is long past, but the cultural expressions of that era are part of Japan's national heritage.

photo: Corbis

Dancers were among the favorite subjects of the early ukiyo-e masters.

Name _____ **Date** _____

GRAPHIC ORGANIZER: Summary Frames

Use these Summary Frames to depict and describe events leading to the development and decline of the feudal system in Japan. For supporting resources, go to Power and Change in Asia, Africa, and the Americas > Japan and Korea > Japanese Society > Explore > Emperor, Shogun, and Daimyo.

Name _____ Date _____

GRAPHIC ORGANIZER: Main Idea Web

Use the smaller circles in this Main Idea Web to identify characteristics of Bushidŏ. Then, next to each bullet point, record facts and details to further describe each characteristic. For supporting resources, go to Power and Change in Asia, Africa, and the Americas > Japan and Korea > Japanese Society > Explore > The Way of the Warrior.

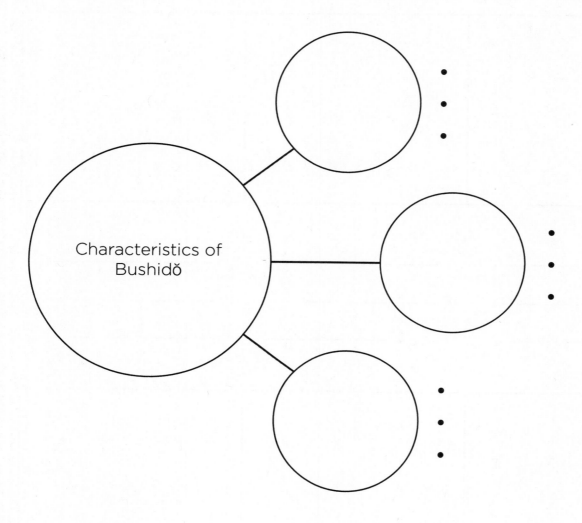

© Discovery Education | www.DiscoveryEducation.com

Name _____ **Date** _____

GRAPHIC ORGANIZER: Comparison Chart

Use this Comparison Chart to compare and contrast the roles and responsibilities of peasants, artisans, and merchants in Japanese society. For supporting resources, go to Power and Change in Asia, Africa, and the Americas > Japan and Korea > Japanese Society > Explore > In Field and Town.

Criteria	Roles	Responsibilities
Peasants		
Artisans		
Merchants		

Name _____ Date _____

EXPLORE: FOCUS QUESTIONS

Using what you learned from the Core Interactive Text, answer each page's focus question:

Emperor, Shogun, and Daimyo
Who held power in feudal Japan?

_____

_____

_____

The End of Feudalism
Why did feudalism in Japan come to an end?

_____

_____

_____

The Way of the Warrior
What was life like for the samurai class in Tokugawa Japan?

_____

_____

_____

Life in the Court of the Daimyo
What was life like for the samurai?

_____

_____

_____

In Field and Town
What was life like for peasants, artisans, and merchants in feudal Japan?

_____

_____

_____

Name _____ Date _____

EXPLORE: FOCUS QUESTIONS *(continued)*

In the Shogun's Court
How did culture develop in Edo under the Tokugawa shogunate?

_____

_____

_____

The Floating World
What sort of culture did the merchant class develop?

_____

_____

_____

A World in 17 Syllables
How did Japanese poets invent haiku?

_____

_____

_____

PROJECTS AND ASSESSMENTS

Explain Activities

ACTIVITY TYPE: DIAGRAM

Japanese Society

In this Mind Map, use at least 10 words from the word bank to create a graphic answer to the Essential Question. You may add any other words or symbols, but you must use all of the starred words. Summarize your map at the bottom and be prepared to present your thinking.

ACTIVITY TYPE: ADVERTISEMENT

Life in Edo

In this activity, you will create an advertisement that shows the benefits of living in the city and addresses worries the samurai and daimyo might have.

ACTIVITY TYPE: SOCIAL STUDIES EXPLANATION

Japanese Society

In this Social Studies Explanation activity, you will use a template to assemble evidence from the sources you have explored. Then, you will write an answer to the Essential Question and defend your answer with supporting evidence.

Elaborate Activities

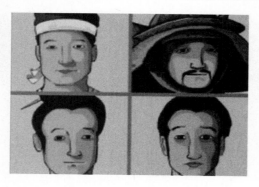

INVESTIGATION TYPE: HISTORICAL PERSPECTIVES

Japanese Feudal Society

Your mission is the get to know four people from four different social classes in feudal Japan. You will then explore the perspectives each person might have on different issues of the day.

photo: Getty Images

ACTIVITY TYPE: SOCRATIC SEMINAR

Bushidŏ: Code of the Samurai

In this Socratic Seminar, you will read excerpts that describe Bushidŏ and then complete a discussion to craft your response to the question: What aspects of Bushidŏ would work well for training soldiers today, and what aspects would not?

PROJECTS AND ASSESSMENTS *(continued)*

photo: Getty Images

ACTIVITY TYPE: YOU AS ARTIST

Ukiyo-e Woodblock Prints

In this activity, you will analyze and compare several ukiyo-e prints and view video segments about this art form. Then, you will create artworks that are similar in style to ukiyo-e prints.

photo: Library of Congress

ACTIVITY TYPE: DOCUMENT-BASED INVESTIGATION

Japanese Society

In this Document-Based Investigation, you will analyze source materials and investigate this question: How did Japanese art reflect the different levels of Japanese society?

Evaluate Activities

BRIEF-CONSTRUCTED RESPONSE (BCR)

Japanese Society

EXTENDED-CONSTRUCTED RESPONSE (ECR)

Japanese Society

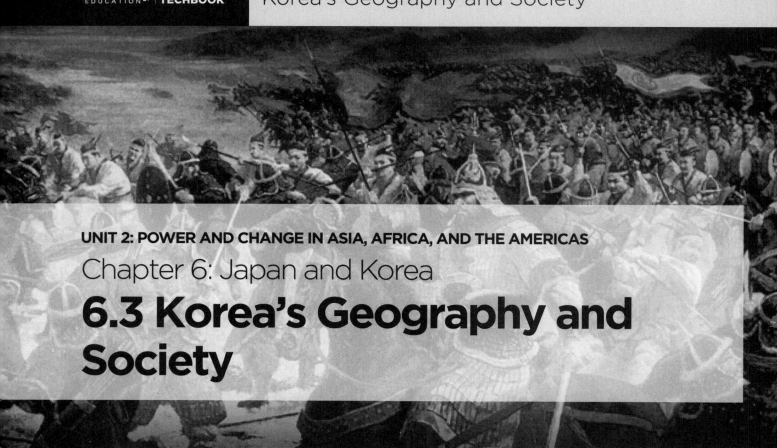

UNIT 2: POWER AND CHANGE IN ASIA, AFRICA, AND THE AMERICAS

Chapter 6: Japan and Korea

6.3 Korea's Geography and Society

LESSON OVERVIEW

Lesson Objectives:

By the end of this lesson, you should be able to:

- Locate the boundaries, important cities, and bodies of water of Korea on a map.
- Analyze how the geography of the region shaped the way of life of the people living there.
- Explain the importance of Mongol rule on Korean society.
- Explain how Korea has served as a link between China and Japan.

Key Vocabulary

absolute monarchy, Buddhism, celadon, China, Chosŏn, Chosŏn dynasty, Confucianism, Europe, Han dynasty, Japan, Johannes Gutenberg, Koguryŏ, Korea, Koryŏ, Mongols, Neo-Confucianism, Paekche, Silk Road, Silla, Taoism, Wang Kon, yangban

Lesson Essential Question:

How did physical location impact life in ancient Korea?

FLASHCARDS

1 Korea's Location

Korea is a peninsula bordered to the west, south, and east by seas and to the north by China and Russia.

- The Amnok and Tumen Rivers flow from Mount Paektu. The Amnok River separates Korea from China.
- To the east, the Sea of Japan lies between Korea and Japan.
- Rivers such as the Han, Kum, Naktong, and Somjin are important to commerce in the western and southern parts of Korea.
- Korea was invaded several times by China.
- Chinese influence played an important role in Korean culture.

Why Does It Matter?

Korea's location between two powerful nations, Japan and China, played a key role in its history and culture for hundreds of years.

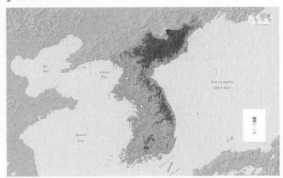

photo: Discovery Education

Korea's location between two powerful nations played an important role in its history.

2 Mongol Rule

The Mongols invaded Korea in 1231.

- Korea fought back for nearly 30 years, but the Mongols finally took control in 1259.
- New ideas and goods flowed to and from Korea as a result of the Mongol-controlled Silk Road.
- Korea perfected movable metal type 200 years before Gutenberg in Europe.
- The Koryŏ dynasty ended in 1392, after years of resisting the Mongols and signing a peace treaty that altered its structure.

Why Does It Matter?

Some of Korea's greatest accomplishments took place while it was under Mongol rule. The changes that took place in Korea during this time set the stage for an even more prosperous period in its history.

photo: Pixabay

The Mongols conquered Korea in 1259, but the time under Mongol rule was a prosperous one for Korea.

FLASHCARDS *(continued)*

3 ▸ Link for Japan and China

Situated between China and Japan, Korea has served as a link between the two nations.

- China invented movable type; Korea perfected it; and Japanese armies brought it to Japan.

- In 1592, Japan invaded Korea to use it as a launching point for an invasion of China. Korea joined forces with China and repelled the Japanese in 1598.

Why Does It Matter?

Japan's desire to claim Korea never faded, and in the 1900s Japan would cause the most drastic changes to Korea.

photo: Los Angeles County Museum of Art (www.lacma.org)

Japan's occupation of Korea led to an exchange of cultures between the civilizations.

Name _____ **Date** _____

GRAPHIC ORGANIZER: Main Idea Web

Use this Main Idea Web to record information about Korea's geography. For supporting resources, go to Power and Change in Asia, Africa, and the Americas > Japan and Korea > Korea's Geography and Society > Explore > Korea's Geography.

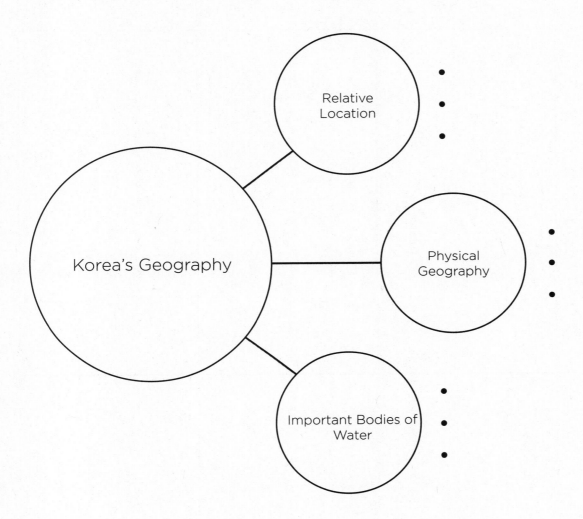

Name _____ **Date** _____

GRAPHIC ORGANIZER: Comparison Chart

Use this Comparison Chart to compare and contrast the Three Kingdoms. For supporting resources, go to Power and Change in Asia, Africa, and the Americas > Japan and Korea > Korea's Geography and Society > Explore > Old Chosŏn.

Criteria	Koguryŏ	Paekche	Silla
Location			
Cultural Characteristics			

Name _____ **Date** _____

GRAPHIC ORGANIZER: Main Idea Web

Use this Main Idea Web to record information about the Koryŏ dynasty. For supporting resources, go to Power and Change in Asia, Africa, and the Americas > Japan and Korea > Korea's Geography and Society > Explore > Koguryŏ's Korea.

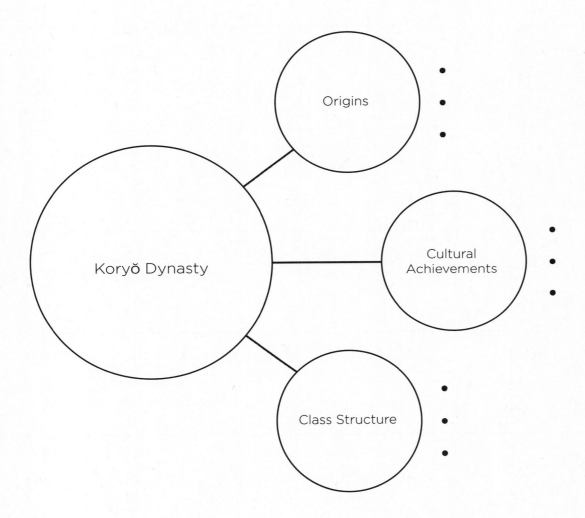

Name _____ Date _____

GRAPHIC ORGANIZER: GREASES Chart

Use this GREASES chart to highlight the important aspects of the Chosŏn Dynasty. For supporting resources, go to Power and Change in Asia, Africa, and the Americas > Japan and Korea > Korea's Geography and Society > Explore > New Chosŏn.

Government	
Religion	
Economic	
Art & Architecture	
Science & Technology	
Environment	
Social & Cultural Values	

Name _____ **Date** _____

EXPLORE: FOCUS QUESTIONS

Using what you learned from the Core Interactive Text, answer each page's focus question:

Korea's Geography
Where is Korea located?

_____

_____

_____

Old Chosŏn
How were Korea's earliest days influenced by China?

_____

_____

_____

United Under Silla
What role did Buddhism play in Silla's Korea?

_____

_____

_____

Koguryŏ's Korea
How did Korea's next dynasty come into power?

_____

_____

_____

Koryŏ Society
What was the social structure during the Koryŏ Dynasty?

_____

_____

_____

Name _____ Date _____

EXPLORE: FOCUS QUESTIONS *(continued)*

Enter the Mongols

How did Korea thrive in spite of invasion?

_____
_____
_____

New Chosŏn

How did Korea change after Mongol rule?

_____
_____
_____

PROJECTS AND ASSESSMENTS

Explain Activities

ACTIVITY TYPE: MOVIE TRAILER

Korea's Geography and Society

In this activity, you will create a movie trailer about how one of the following influenced Korea: the Koryŏ dynasty, the Mongol invasions, or the Chinese invasions. The movie trailer should help the audience understand what the documentary is about and become excited to see how the information unfolds in the movie.

ACTIVITY TYPE: QUICK WRITE

The Influence of China and Japan

In this Quick Write, you will choose to write about how either Japan or China has influenced Korea's political and cultural development.

ACTIVITY TYPE: SOCIAL STUDIES EXPLANATION

Korea's Geography and Society

In this Social Studies Explanation activity, you will use a template to assemble evidence from the sources you have explored. Then, you will write an answer to the Essential Question and defend your answer with supporting evidence.

Elaborate Activities

photo: Gettty Images

INVESTIGATION TYPE: TIMELINE MAP

Korea's Geography and Society

How did physical location affect life in ancient Korea? In this investigation, you will use the Timeline Map interactive tool to examine the development of civilization in ancient Korea and explain the influence of physical location on these developments.

ACTIVITY TYPE: YOU AS ARTIST

A Korean Folktale

In this activity, you will read a folktale by Pang Im, a writer from 17th-century Korea. In this folktale, Pang Im tells a story of how one village was saved from the destruction of the Manchu forces, shown in the illustration. After reading the folktale, you will create an illustration of the folktale's events as a graphic novel.

photo: Los Angeles County Museum of Art (www.lacma.org)

PROJECTS AND ASSESSMENTS *(continued)*

photo: Discovery Education

ACTIVITY TYPE: CURRENT EVENTS CONNECTION

Korea and Imperialism

In this activity, imagine you have been invited to participate in a round-table discussion on imperialism. You will write a statement explaining how past imperialism still affects Korea today.

photo: Pixabay

ACTIVITY TYPE: DOCUMENT-BASED INVESTIGATION

Korea's Geography and Society

In this Document-Based Investigation, you will analyze source materials and investigate this question: To what extent did Chinese traditions influence Korean culture?

Evaluate Activities

BRIEF-CONSTRUCTED RESPONSE (BCR)

Korea's Geography and Society

EXTENDED-CONSTRUCTED RESPONSE (ECR)

Korea's Geography and Society

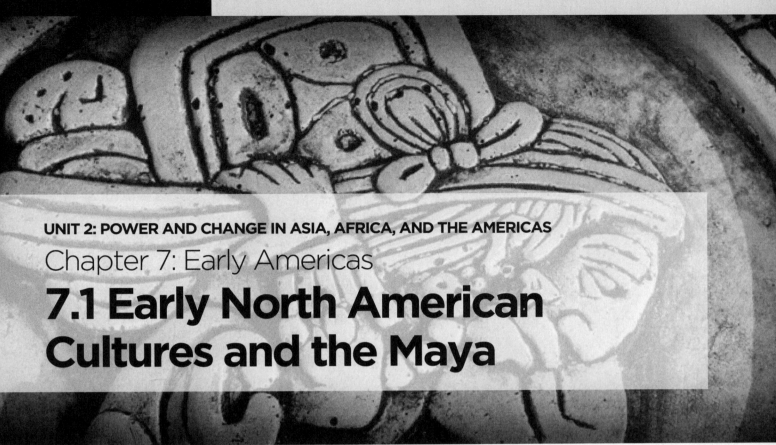

photo: Getty Images

UNIT 2: POWER AND CHANGE IN ASIA, AFRICA, AND THE AMERICAS

Chapter 7: Early Americas

7.1 Early North American Cultures and the Maya

LESSON OVERVIEW

Lesson Objectives:

By the end of this lesson, you should be able to:

- **Locate the physical features and early American civilizations on a map of the Americas.**
- **Describe how the geography of the region shaped the way of life of the people living there.**
- **Describe Mayan culture and scientific innovations.**

Lesson Essential Question:

How did physical geography shape the early societies of the Americas?

Key Vocabulary

Amazon River, Andes, Atlantic Ocean, Aztec, Central Plateau, Chichén Itzá, Christopher Columbus, Classic Period, climate, codex, colonization, conquistador, Copan, Egypt, Inca, indentured servant, infrastructure, La Venta, maize, Maya, mestizo, Mexico, Middle America, Nile River, Northwest Passage, Olmec, Peru, polytheism, South America, stela, steppe, terrace farming, Toltec, treaty, Yucatán Peninsula, ziggurat

FLASHCARDS

1 ▸

Geography of the Americas

Pre-Columbian peoples lived throughout the continents of North and South America and in Central America.

- The Maya lived in the highlands of southern Mexico and the lowlands of Central America.
- Mound-building peoples lived in North America.
- Cliff dwellers lived in the southwestern United States.

Why Does It Matter?

The geography of the Americas played an important role in the development of the early people who settled there. As each people adapted to its environment, unique cultures developed. These cultures gave rise to the tribes found by the Europeans when they came to the Americas.

photo: Pixabay

Fertile farmland for growing crops in the Americas helped make agriculture an important part of the civilizations that developed there.

2 ▸

The Mayan Empire

The development of the Mayan culture was shaped by the geography and climate of Central America and Mexico.

- The Olmec were cultural ancestors of the Maya.
- The Maya built a large road system connecting them to other cities and civilizations.
- Mayan farmers practiced terraced agriculture. Crops included corn, cacao beans, and rubber.
- Each Mayan city was ruled by a separate leader, and they often fought each other.
- The Maya developed a complex calendar system, a number system, a writing system, and a language that influenced modern languages still spoken in Central America and Mexico.

Why Does It Matter?

The Maya developed many of their unique characteristics because of their geographical location.

photo: Jupiterimages Corporation

The Maya built cities throughout Central America and Mexico, where these city ruins are located.

FLASHCARDS *(continued)*

3 Culture and Innovations of the Maya

The Maya developed and improved upon a number of innovations in the areas of math, astronomy, and language.

- The Maya developed a very accurate system of two intersecting calendars. Other Mesoamerican societies adopted this system.
- The Maya adapted a number system originally developed by the Zapotec, which used only three symbols but could be used to solve complex equations.
- The Maya built palaces, sculptures, and observatories used for astronomy.
- The Maya kept written records on stone stelae and codices.
- Variations of the original Mayan languages are spoken by many people in Central America today.

Why Does It Matter?

The central location of the Mayan people, along with the warm and fertile climate, allowed them to share both goods and ideas with neighboring peoples. This also allowed their innovations to survive.

photo: Pixabay

A stone carving shows the written language of the ancient Maya.

Name _____ **Date** _____

GRAPHIC ORGANIZER: Map of South America

Use this Map to label and describe geographic features in Mesoamerica. For supporting resources, go to Power and Change in Asia, Africa, and the Americas > Early Americas > Early North American Cultures and the Maya > Explore > Geography of Mesoamerica.

Name _____ Date _____

GRAPHIC ORGANIZER: Three-Way Venn Diagram

Use this Three-Way Venn Diagram to compare the Maya with the Ancestral Pueblo (Anasazi) and Cahokia (mound builders). For supporting resources, go to Power and Change in Asia, Africa, and the Americas > Early Americas > Early North American Cultures and the Maya > Explore > Nations of the Pre-Columbian Americas.

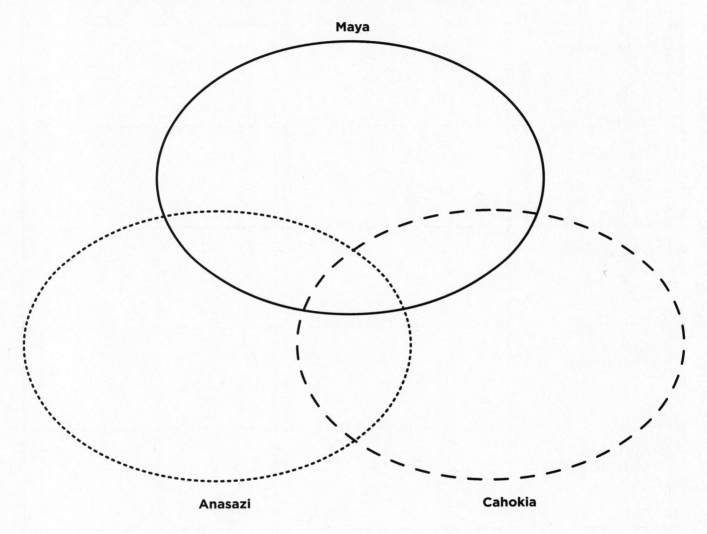

Name _____ Date _____

GRAPHIC ORGANIZER: GREASES Chart

Use this GREASES Chart to record details about the Mayan civilization. For supporting resources, go to Power and Change in Asia, Africa, and the Americas > Early Americas > Early North American Cultures and the Maya > Explore > Mayan Agriculture.

	What I See	My Conclusions
Government		
Religion		
Economic		
Art & Architecture		
Science & Technology		
Environment		
Social & Cultural Values		

Name _____ **Date** _____

EXPLORE: FOCUS QUESTIONS

Using what you learned from the Core Interactive Text, answer each page's focus question:

Geography of Mesoamerica
What are the important geographical features of the Americas?

_____

_____

_____

Nations of the Pre-Columbian Americas
How did the Toltec and Olmec influence Mesoamerican culture?

_____

_____

_____

Ancient Builders
How did geography shape the development of early North American people?

_____

_____

_____

The Maya
What were the characteristics of the Mayan civilization?

_____

_____

_____

Mayan Agriculture
What role did agriculture play in the Mayan civilization?

_____

_____

_____

Mayan Religion
What was the religious culture of the Maya?

_____

_____

_____

Name _____ Date _____

EXPLORE: FOCUS QUESTIONS *(continued)*

A Decentralized Nation
How did the Maya organize their society?

_____
_____
_____
_____

A Society of Thinkers
What scientific innovations did the Maya develop?

_____
_____
_____
_____

Language and Math
What cultural innovations did the Mayan civilization develop?

_____
_____
_____

PROJECTS AND ASSESSMENTS

Explain Activities

ACTIVITY TYPE: DIAGRAM

Comparing Civilizations

In this activity, you will use a Venn diagram to compare and contrast the Olmec civilization with one of the four early river valley civilizations (Nile, Tigris-Euphrates, Indus, or Yellow). On the back, write a short paragraph describing the similarities and differences between the Olmec and your chosen civilization.

ACTIVITY TYPE: QUICK WRITE

Mayan Innovations

In this activity, you will create an advertisement for one of the ancient Mayan innovations or contributions.

ACTIVITY TYPE: VISUALIZATION

Mesoamerican Geography

In this Visualization activity, you choose a major geographical feature for the Anasazi, Cahokian, and Maya, and then explain how the geographic feature helped define each society.

ACTIVITY TYPE: SOCIAL STUDIES EXPLANATION

Early North American Cultures and the Maya

In this Social Studies Explanation activity, you will use a template to assemble evidence from the sources you have explored. Then, you will write an answer to the Essential Question and defend your answer with supporting evidence.

Elaborate Activities

photo: Getty Images

INVESTIGATION TYPE: SOURCE ANALYSIS

The Mayan Calendars

What role did the Mayan calendars play in the daily lives of people? Analyze the Haab calendar and its importance in the lives of the Maya people.

PROJECTS AND ASSESSMENTS *(continued)*

photo: IRC

ACTIVITY TYPE: PITCH YOUR IDEA

Math of the Maya

In this activity, you will create a presentation to give before a foreign leader explaining how the mathematical innovations of the ancient Maya could improve his kingdom.

photo: Getty Images

ACTIVITY TYPE: STUDENT SLEUTH

Mayan Ball Games

In this activity, you will analyze photographs of ball courts and players, a myth about ball games, and descriptions of the game. Then, you will write the narrative script for the section of the documentary on Mayan ball games, in which you describe the game and its purposes.

photo: Paul Fuqua

ACTIVITY TYPE: DOCUMENT-BASED INVESTIGATION

Mayan Beliefs

In this activity, you will create an exhibit for a museum (or online museum) that shows visitors what Mayan beliefs and rituals reveal about their geography and society. Or, you can create a documentary in which you identify what Mayan beliefs and rituals reveal about their geography and society.

Evaluate Activities

BRIEF-CONSTRUCTED RESPONSE (BCR)

Early North American Cultures and the Maya

EXTENDED-CONSTRUCTED RESPONSE (ECR)

Early North American Cultures and the Maya

photo: IRC

LESSON OVERVIEW

UNIT 2: POWER AND CHANGE IN ASIA, AFRICA, AND THE AMERICAS

Chapter 7: Early Americas
7.2 The Aztec Empire

Lesson Objectives:

By the end of this lesson, you should be able to:

- Explain the rise and growth of the Aztec Empire.
- Analyze the political and social structure of Aztec civilization.

Lesson Essential Question:

How did the Aztec Empire become so powerful with such speed?

Key Vocabulary

Aztec, Aztec Empire, conquistador, Hernán Cortés, Itzcóatl, Lake Texcoco, Maya, Mexica, Mexico, Montezuma, polytheism, social class, tribute

FLASHCARDS

1 A Triple Alliance

The Aztec civilization was located in central Mexico. It consisted of tribes that formed a Triple Alliance. They were defeated by Spanish conquistadores in the 1500s.

- The alliance was made up of tribes from the cities of Tenochtitlán, Texcoco, and Tlacopan.
- The Mexica were the tribe that became known as the Aztec. They would eventually build the Aztec Empire.
- Following their belief in a religious prophecy, the Mexica settled near Lake Texcoco.

Why Does It Matter?

The Aztec civilization was a grouping of several tribes. The political alliance allowed them to band together to defeat other tribes. They were able to expand their empire throughout the region and become a large, wealthy, and advanced civilization.

photo: Getty's Open Content Program

The Aztec conquered other tribes and lands to obtain tributes: items such as cocoa, cotton, feathers, and cloth. This wealth helped them to expand their empire.

2 Daily Life in the Empire

In the divided Aztec society, people had different roles. All children were educated, but at different levels and in different subjects. The gods of the culture were greatly respected. The society was eventually conquered by Spanish explorers.

- Upper-class children were schooled to be government officials or temple priests.
- All boys were trained to be warriors.
- Girls were trained in domestic skills like cooking and sewing.
- The Aztec believed in human sacrifice to their gods.
- Montezuma expanded the Aztec empire and made improvements to the city of Tenochtitlán.
- Cortés was a Spanish explorer who claimed Mexico for Spain.

Why Does It Matter?

The split education system meant that no one could rise above his or her class, with the exception of boys whose parents were skilled warriors or wealthy merchants, or individuals who excelled in battle. All children were schooled for their roles in society. Religion played an important role in everyday life. Religious ceremonies were performed based on the calendar, and large amounts of resources were dedicated to building temples and conducting religious ceremonies. Conquered people had to pay tribute to the Aztec emperor, which caused some unrest and rebellion in the empire. This unrest would pave the way for the success of outside conquest.

photo: Library of Congress

The Aztec had a structured society. Class and sex determined an individual's role in the society.

Name _____ **Date** _____

GRAPHIC ORGANIZER: Timeline

Use this Timeline to record important events and dates in the rise of the Aztec Empire. For supporting resources, go to Power and Change in Asia, Africa, and the Americas > Early Americas > The Aztec Empire > Explore > The Earliest Days of Mexico.

1100 CE   1600 CE

◆——◆

Name _____ **Date** _____

GRAPHIC ORGANIZER: Main Idea Web

Use this Main Idea Web to highlight the important aspects of Aztec religion and culture. For supporting resources, go to Power and Change in Asia, Africa, and the Americas > Early Americas > The Aztec Empire > Explore > Religion of the Aztec.

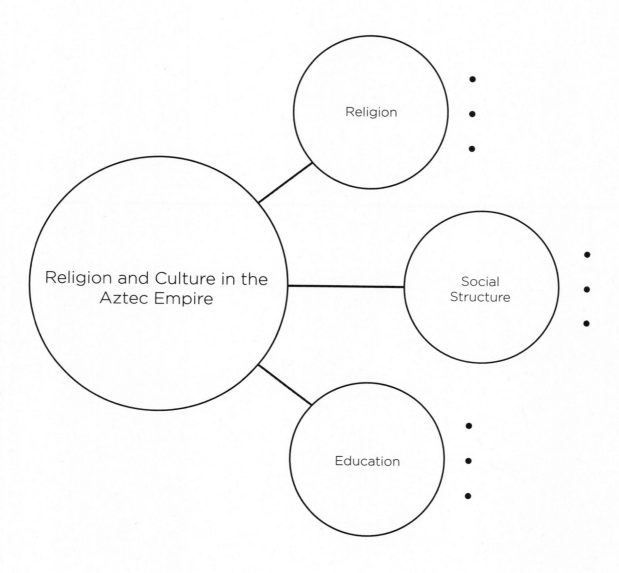

Name _____ **Date** _____

GRAPHIC ORGANIZER: Comparison Chart

Use this Comparison Chart to compare and contrast the Aztec and Spanish civilizations. In the final column, record questions you have about these societies and how they interacted. For supporting resources, go to Power and Change in Asia, Africa, and the Americas > Early Americas > The Aztec Empire > Explore > Montezuma and Cortés.

Criteria	Aztec	Spanish	Questions
Notes			

Name _____ Date _____

EXPLORE: FOCUS QUESTIONS

Using what you learned from the Core Interactive Text, answer each page's focus question:

The Earliest Days of Mexico
Who were the Aztec people?

_____
_____
_____

The Aztec Build an Empire
How did the Aztec people become united?

_____
_____
_____

Further Expansion
How did the Aztec Empire continue to expand under the rule of Itzcóatl?

_____
_____
_____

Religion of the Aztec
What role did religion play in Aztec society?

_____
_____
_____

Daily Life in the Empire
What was life like in the Aztec Empire?

_____
_____
_____

Montezuma and Cortés
How were the Spanish explorers initially received by the new emperor?

_____
_____
_____

PROJECTS AND ASSESSMENTS

Explain Activities

ACTIVITY TYPE: DIAGRAM

The Aztec Empire

In this activity, you will use at least 10 words from the Word Bank to create a graphic answer to the Essential Question.

ACTIVITY TYPE: MOVIE TRAILER

The Aztec Story

In this activity, you will create a movie trailer for a film about an event in Aztec history from before 1500 CE.

ACTIVITY TYPE: SOCIAL STUDIES EXPLANATION

The Aztec Empire

In this Social Studies Explanation activity, you will use a template to assemble evidence from the sources you have explored. Then, you will write an answer to the Essential Question and defend your answer with supporting evidence.

Elaborate Activities

photo: The World Factbook: Central Intelligence Agency

INVESTIGATION TYPE: SOURCE ANALYSIS

The Codex Mendoza

What does the Codex Mendoza contain, and how does it depict elements of Aztec society? Your mission is to analyze a page from the Codex Mendoza to learn about the Aztec myth describing the founding of Tenochtitlán.

photo: Getty Images

ACTIVITY TYPE: ROLE PLAY

Life in Aztec Mexico

In this activity, you will work with a group to create a museum exhibit showing daily life as a member of your assigned social class and city—either Tenochtitlán or the neighboring Ocotelolco, Tizatlan, Quiahuiztlan, or Tepeticpac tribes.

PROJECTS AND ASSESSMENTS *(continued)*

photo: Getty Images

ACTIVITY TYPE: EXPRESS YOUR OPINION

War or Tribute?

Imagine that you are an adviser to a local ruler in an area just outside the Aztec Empire. This ruler knows that soon, Aztec ambassadors will come to his land and demand that he pay tribute to the empire. When they do, he will have to decide whether to try to stay independent or to give in and send tribute to Tenochtitlán. In this activity, you will write a speech to give to your ruler, explaining what you think he should do, and why.

photo: Library of Congresss

ACTIVITY TYPE: DOCUMENT-BASED INVESTIGATION

The Aztec and Violence

In this activity, you will write a letter either supporting or arguing against Professor Know-It-All's book, "Everything There Is to Know About the Aztec Empire," which claims that the Aztec were bloodthirsty conquerors who ruled their empire through physical violence. Alternately, you will create a documentary presentation called "The Real Aztec," in which you deliver an argument for or against Professor Know-It-All's interpretation.

Evaluate Activities

BRIEF-CONSTRUCTED RESPONSE (BCR)

The Aztec Empire

EXTENDED-CONSTRUCTED RESPONSE (ECR)

The Aztec Empire

Discovery EDUCATION | SOCIAL STUDIES TECHBOOK.

UNIT 2: POWER AND CHANGE IN ASIA, AFRICA, AND THE AMERICAS

Chapter 7: Early Americas
7.3 The Inca Empire

photo: Paul Fuqua

LESSON OVERVIEW

Lesson Objectives:

By the end of this lesson, you should be able to:

- **Analyze the impact of physical geography on Incan culture.**
- **Describe the Incan political and social structures.**

Key Vocabulary

Andes, Cuzco, emperor, Francisco Pizarro, guano, Inca, irrigation, llama, Machu Picchu, Pachacuti, Peru, South America, terrace farming

Lesson Essential Question:

How did the Inca Empire maintain power across such a challenging geographic location?

FLASHCARDS

A People in the Clouds

The physical geography of the Inca Empire impacted its people in many ways.

- The Inca used terrace farming on the steep hillsides of the Andes.
- The Inca created a system of roads, sometimes linked by suspension bridges, which aided communication, travel, and trade.
- The city of Machu Picchu is an excellent example of Incan engineering and architecture.

Why Does It Matter?

The mountainous terrain and huge amount of land occupied by the Inca Empire made it a challenge to keep the empire united.

photo: Pixabay

The Andes Mountain chain is over 4,000 miles long. What kinds of challenges would be the result of living in a place like this?

2 An Empire United

The Inca Empire was characterized by unique political and social structures.

- Pachacuti was the first emperor to expand the empire aggressively.
- Cuzco was the Incan capital, but regional capitals in the four quarters of the empire helped administer the Incan government.
- The Inca conquered many regions with their strong army, but other regions joined the empire willingly after being invited by the emperor.
- The Incan government collected tribute in the form of gold and silver from local governments.

Why Does It Matter?

The Incan emperors conquered huge expanses of land. Regional governments helped the emperors keep control of an empire as large as the Atlantic Coast states in the United States.

photo: Library of Congress

These stone foundations pictured in modern-day Cuzco were created by their Incan ancestors. Fitted without mortar, they are a testimony to the engineering skill of the Inca.

Name _____ Date _____

GRAPHIC ORGANIZER: GREASES Chart

Use this GREASES Chart to record details about the Inca Empire. For supporting resources, go to Power and Change in Asia, Africa, and the Americas > Early Americas > The Inca Empire > Explore > Geography of the Inca Empire.

Government	
Religion	
Economic	
Art & **Architecture**	
Science & **Technology**	
Environment	
Social & **Cultural Values**	

Name _____ **Date** _____

GRAPHIC ORGANIZER: Problem/Solution Chart

Use this Problem/Solution Chart to describe the challenges that the Inca faced as a result of the physical geography of the region (problems) and the ways in which the Inca met those challenges (solutions). For supporting resources, go to Power and Change in Asia, Africa, and the Americas > Early Americas > The Inca Empire > Explore > Farming in the Andes.

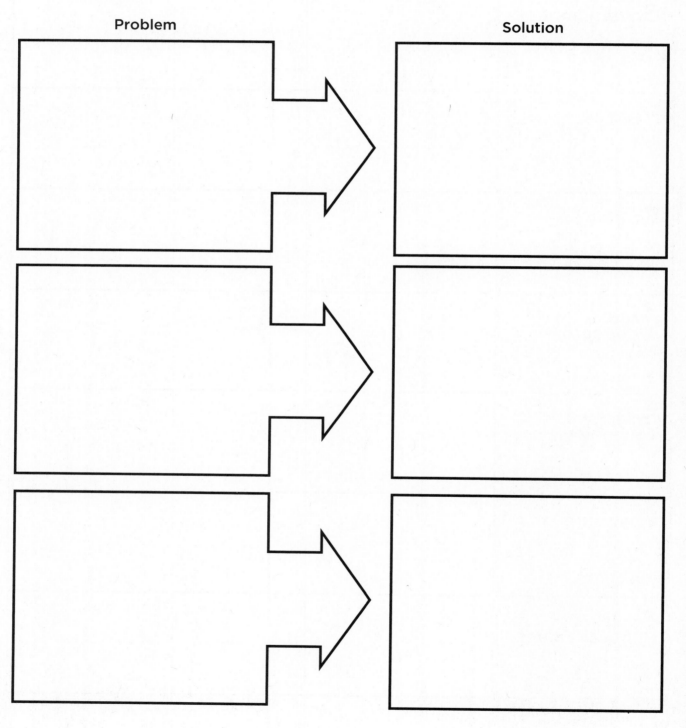

Problem   **Solution**

Name _____ **Date** _____

GRAPHIC ORGANIZER: Problem/Solution Chart *(continued)*

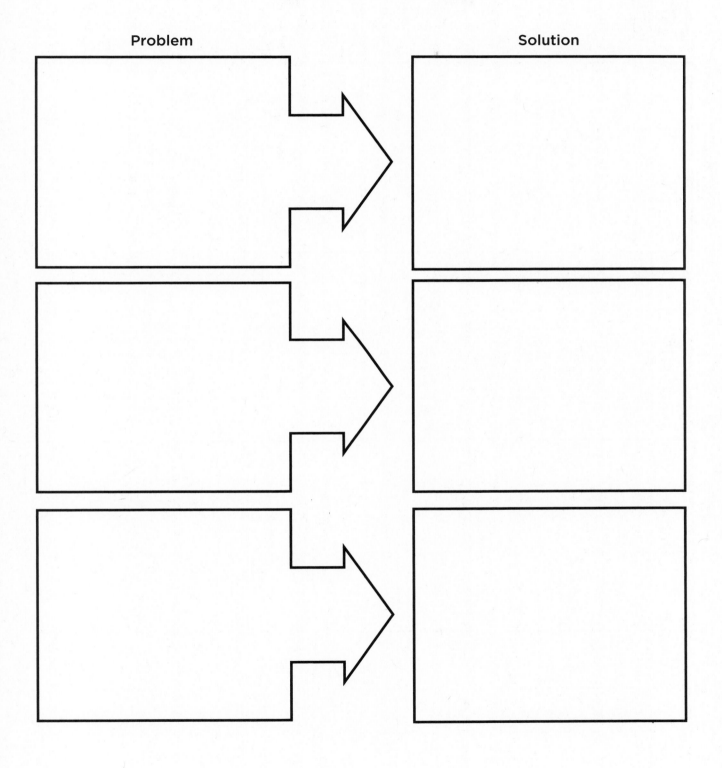

Problem   Solution

Name _____ **Date** _____

GRAPHIC ORGANIZER: Summary Frames

Use these Summary Frames to summarize the major events in the expansion of the Inca Empire. For supporting resources, go to Power and Change in Asia, Africa, and the Americas > Early Americas > The Inca Empire > Explore > Building the Empire.

_____ _____ _____

_____ _____ _____

_____ _____ _____

_____ _____ _____

_____ _____ _____

_____ _____ _____

Name _____ **Date** _____

GRAPHIC ORGANIZER: Main Idea Web

Use this Main Idea Web to record the major aspects of the Inca Empire's political structure and organization. For supporting resources, go to Power and Change in Asia, Africa, and the Americas > Early Americas > The Inca Empire > Explore > The Political Structure of the Inca.

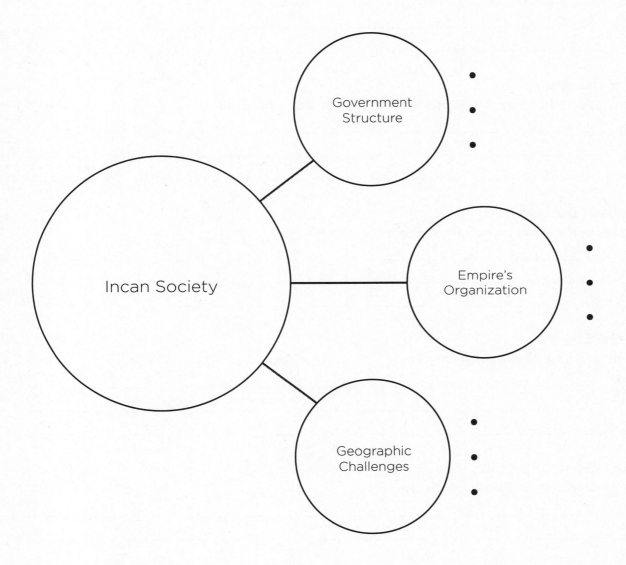

Name _____ Date _____

EXPLORE: FOCUS QUESTIONS

Using what you learned from the Core Interactive Text, answer each page's focus question:

Geography of the Inca Empire

Where was the Inca Empire located?

_____
_____
_____

Farming in the Andes

How did the physical geography of their empire impact Incan agriculture?

_____
_____
_____

Highways and Byways

How did geography impact travel throughout the Inca Empire?

_____
_____
_____

Building the Empire

How did the Inca Empire expand its holdings?

_____
_____
_____

The Political Structure of the Inca

What was the structure of the Incan government?

_____
_____
_____

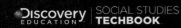

Name _____ Date _____

EXPLORE: FOCUS QUESTIONS *(continued)*

An Organized Empire
How did the Inca organize their growing empire?

_____

_____

_____

The Mystery of Machu Picchu
What does the Inca city Machu Picchu reveal about Incan architecture and engineering?

_____

_____

_____

PROJECTS AND ASSESSMENTS

Explain Activities

ACTIVITY TYPE: DIAGRAM

The Inca Empire

In this activity, use at least 10 words from the Word Bank to create a graphic response to the Essential Question. You must use all the starred words in your response. Summarize your map at the bottom and be prepared to present your thinking.

ACTIVITY TYPE: QUICK WRITE

The Inca Empire

In this Quick Write activity, you will write a paragraph explaining several methods Incan rulers used to effectively expand and govern their large and culturally diverse empire, based on the four specific examples of evidence you selected.

ACTIVITY TYPE: SOCIAL STUDIES EXPLANATION

The Inca Empire

In this Social Studies Explanation activity, you will use a template to assemble evidence from the sources you have explored. Then, you will write an answer to the Essential Question and defend your answer with supporting evidence.

Elaborate Activities

photo: The World Factbook: Central Intelligence Agency

INVESTIGATION TYPE: MAP-GUIDED INQUIRY

The Inca Empire

How did geography influence the development of the powerful Incan Empire in South America? In this investigation, you will use the Map-Guided Inquiry interactive tool to describe the culture and government that emerged in the Incan Empire.

photo: Getty Images

ACTIVITY TYPE: CURRENT EVENTS CONNECTION

Incan Roads and U.S. Highways

In this activity, you will research Incan roads and the highway system in the United States. You will then create a graphic organizer comparing the two and write an essay about their similarities and differences.

PROJECTS AND ASSESSMENTS *(continued)*

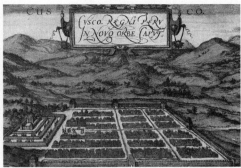

photo: Getty Images

ACTIVITY TYPE: MAKE A MODEL

The Inca Empire

In this activity, you will use a number of resources to learn about the city of Cuzco. You will then use what you have learned to create a model that explains how the city made use of natural resources and how the elements of the city demonstrated the social order and other aspects of Incan society.

photo: Paul Fuqua

ACTIVITY TYPE: DOCUMENT-BASED INVESTIGATION

The Inca Empire

In this activity, imagine you are a citizen of the Inca Empire. Write either a journal entry describing the physical geography of your land and explaining how your people have adapted to the region or a newspaper article describing the physical geography of the land and how the Inca are building their empire there.

Evaluate Activities

BRIEF-CONSTRUCTED RESPONSE (BCR)

The Inca Empire

EXTENDED-CONSTRUCTED RESPONSE (ECR)

The Inca Empire

SOCIAL STUDIES TECHBOOK

photo: Paul Fuqua

UNIT 2: POWER AND CHANGE IN ASIA, AFRICA, AND THE AMERICAS

Chapter 8: African Empires

8.1 Geography of Africa

LESSON OVERVIEW

Lesson Objectives:

By the end of this lesson, you should be able to:

- **Locate the boundaries, important cities, and bodies of water of Africa on a map.**
- **Describe how the geography of the region shaped the way of life of the people living there.**

Lesson Essential Question:

How did the geography of Africa affect its settlement patterns and commerce?

Key Vocabulary

Aksum, Atlantic Ocean, Bantu, Bantu Migrations, Bartolomeu Dias, Congo River, Congo River Basin, desert, East Africa, Ethiopia, Ghana, Giza, Great Rift Valley, Great Zimbabwe, Indian Ocean, Kalahari Desert, Kingdom of Benin, Kush, Mali, Mogadishu, Mombasa, Morocco, Mount Kilamanjaro, Niger River, Nile River, nomadic, Sahara Desert, Sahel, savanna, Sofala, Sub-Saharan Africa, Timbuktu, trade, Zambezi River, Zanzibar

FLASHCARDS

1 African Geography

Africa is a large continent surrounded by oceans and seas. It is divided in two by the Sahara Desert. Sub-Saharan Africa is the region that lies south of the Sahara Desert.

- **Africa is bordered by two major oceans, the Atlantic and the Indian, and several smaller seas, the Red Sea and the Mediterranean Sea.**
- **Africa has four major rivers, the Nile, the Niger, the Congo, and the Zambezi. Although all of the rivers are navigable in places, near the coast they fall through a series of cataracts, which prevents boats from traveling from the coast to the interior.**
- **Sub-Saharan Africa has four climate zones: desert, semiarid or Sahel, savanna or grasslands, and tropical forests. The climate zones mirror each other across the equator.**
- **Sub-Saharan Africa saw many cities develop during the medieval period. Some of these cities, such as Aksum, Djenne, and Ile-Ife, developed as trading cities. Others, such as Great Zimbabwe, developed due to the rich natural resources they contained.**

Why Does It Matter?

Africa's geography shaped the continent and its ancient, as well as more recent, history.

photo: Pixabay

This is an aerial photo of the Niger Inland Delta. Its annual floods make the land surrounding the river fertile and good for agriculture.

2 Farming, Herding, and Trade

The lives of people in Sub-Saharan Africa have been shaped by their environment. People migrating from one climate zone to another have had to adapt.

- **The Bantu migrations were a movement of people from West Africa across Sub-Saharan Africa. Historians dispute the reasons why the Bantu migrated. Although the descendants of the Bantu share a language family, their cultures differ widely from ethnic group to ethnic group.**
- **Climate zones have determined how people made a living in Sub-Saharan Africa. In the forests, farmers grew yams, palm trees, and kola trees. In the savannas, farmers grew grain crops. In the semiarid and desert areas, nomadic herders moved from place to place in search of water and food for their animals.**
- **The development of different resources in each climate zone caused trade routes to develop between the climate zones as people traded for things they could not produce themselves.**

Why Does It Matter?

Because Africa contains a rich variety of climates, trade routes helped connect societies that needed resources from one another. These trade routes helped the main empires of Africa to form and grow in power and wealth.

photo: Discovery Education

The savanna is a good place for growing crops such as millet.

Name _____ Date _____

GRAPHIC ORGANIZER: Main Idea Web

Use this Main Idea Web to record characteristics of each geographic feature and list the ways in which each feature helps to shape life in Africa. For supporting resources, go to Power and Change in Asia, Africa, and the Americas > African Empires > Geography of Africa > Explore > Large Rivers and Harsh Deserts.

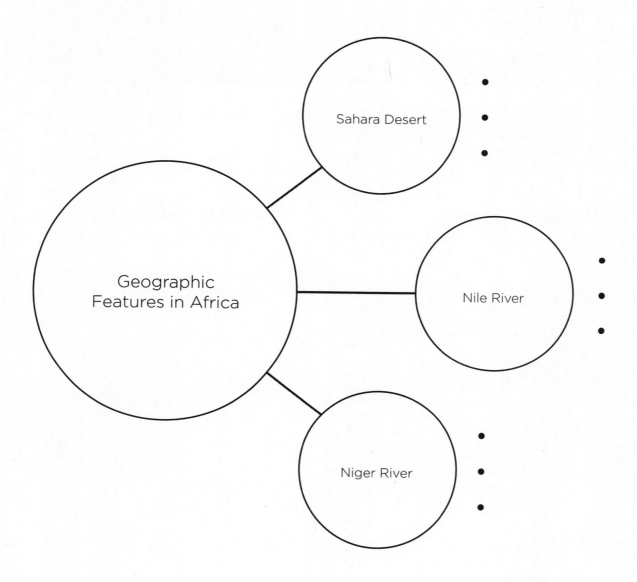

Name _____ **Date** _____

GRAPHIC ORGANIZER: Comparison Chart

Use this Comparison Chart to identify the similarities and differences among the four major climate zones in Sub-Saharan Africa: tropical forest, savannah, semiarid strip, and southern desert. For supporting resources, go to Power and Change in Asia, Africa, and the Americas > African Empires > Geography of Africa > Explore > Climate Zones.

Criteria	Tropical Forest	Savanna	Semiarid Strip	Southern Desert
Description of Climate				
Vegetation				
Plant Life				

Name _____ **Date** _____

GRAPHIC ORGANIZER: Sequencing Chart

Use this Sequencing Chart to plot the progress of the Bantu peoples' migration in Africa. In the left column, list the general time period of each migration event. In the right column, provide a brief description of each event. Start with the earliest migration event discussed. For supporting resources, go to Power and Change in Asia, Africa, and the Americas > African Empires > Geography of Africa > Explore > On the Move.

Time Period	Migration Event

Name _____ **Date** _____

EXPLORE: FOCUS QUESTIONS

Using what you learned from the Core Interactive Text, answer each page's focus question:

Large Rivers and Harsh Deserts
What geographic features shape the continent of Africa?

_____

_____

_____

Climate Zones
What types of vegetation are there in Sub-Saharan Africa?

_____

_____

_____

Making a Living
How did the environment affect the economy of Sub-Saharan Africa?

_____

_____

_____

On the Move
Who were the Bantu?

_____

_____

_____

Trade
Why did trade routes run north and south in Sub-Saharan Africa?

_____

_____

_____

Major Cities
What were the major cities of medieval Africa?

_____

_____

_____

PROJECTS AND ASSESSMENTS

Explain Activities

ACTIVITY TYPE: VISUALIZATION

Geography of Africa

Imagine you are a travel writer and your editor has asked you to create a feature describing the four main climate zones of Sub-Saharan Africa. You will be creating a visual spread for the magazine article.

ACTIVITY TYPE: QUICK WRITE

Geography of Africa

In this Quick Write activity, you will take the perspective of a medieval trader from Aksum, Djenne, Timbuktu, Benin, or Zimbabwe. As that trader, you will reflect on the geographic advantages of your home city.

ACTIVITY TYPE: SOCIAL STUDIES EXPLANATION

Geography of Africa

In this Social Studies Explanation activity, you will use a template to assemble evidence from the sources you have explored. Then, you will write an answer to the Essential Question and defend your answer with supporting evidence.

Elaborate Activities

photo: Discovery Education

INVESTIGATION TYPE: MAP-GUIDED INQUIRY

The Geography of Africa

How did geography influence the settlement and economy of early Africa? In this investigation, you will use the Map-Guided Inquiry interactive tool to examine how early Africa compares to modern Africa on a map.

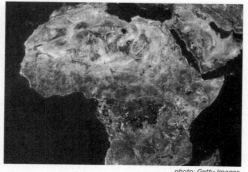

photo: Getty Images

ACTIVITY TYPE: PITCH YOUR IDEA

Building a City in Sub-Saharan Africa

In this activity, you will take on the role of a city planner who has been charged with choosing the best location for a new city.

PROJECTS AND ASSESSMENTS *(continued)*

photo: Getty Images

ACTIVITY TYPE: CURRENT EVENTS
CONNECTION

The Sahel: Yesterday and Today

In this activity, you will explore the Sahel region of Africa in the medieval era (400–1500 CE) and in the present. Then, you will assume the role of a time-traveling investigator and prepare a written report along with a video or slideshow presentation. Your report will compare the benefits and the drawbacks of life on the Sahel during both time periods.

photo: Getty Images

ACTIVITY TYPE: DOCUMENT-BASED
INVESTIGATION

Different Civilizations and Climate Zones

In this Document-Based Investigation, you will compare several climate zones in Sub-Saharan Africa, such as the tropical rainforest, savannah, semiarid strip, and southern desert. You will then create a guidebook for a new gaming platform entitled "Sim-Africa" or prepare a travel log from the perspective of an explorer.

Evaluate Activities

BRIEF-CONSTRUCTED RESPONSE (BCR)

Geography of Africa

EXTENDED-CONSTRUCTED RESPONSE (ECR)

Geography of Africa

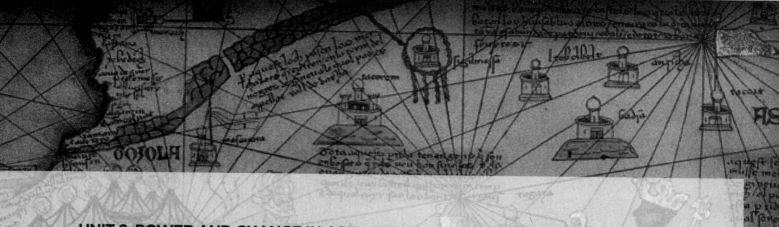

DISCOVERY EDUCATION | SOCIAL STUDIES TECHBOOK

UNIT 2: POWER AND CHANGE IN ASIA, AFRICA, AND THE AMERICAS

Chapter 8: African Empires

8.2 Growth of African Empires

photo: Getty Images

LESSON OVERVIEW

Lesson Objectives:

By the end of this lesson, you should be able to:

- **Trace the growth of the empires of Ghana, Mali, and Songhai.**
- **Describe the cultural, social, economic, and political characteristics of African empires.**

Lesson Essential Question:

How did trade influence the politics and culture of African empires?

Key Vocabulary

Aksum, Arabian Peninsula, Atlantic Ocean, caravan, China, city-state, desert, Egypt, embargo, Ethiopia, Europe, Ghana, Ghana Empire, goods, Great Zimbabwe, Ibn Battuta, Indian Ocean, Indian Subcontinent, Kingdom of Benin, Mali, Mali Empire, Mansa Musa, markets, Mecca, merchant, Mogadishu, Morocco, Muslims, Niger River, North Africa, Nubia, pilgrimage, province, Red Sea, Sahara Desert, Sahel, Songhai, Songhai Empire, Timbuktu, trade, West Africa

FLASHCARDS

1 Empires Rise

In West Africa, three great empires gained power by controlling the gold and salt trades. In combination, these three empires successively controlled the Sahel region of West Africa for more than 900 years.

- Gold, mined in the West Africa forests, was desired by markets in North Africa and Europe. West Africans needed salt from the Sahara Desert to survive in their hot climate. Trade caravans crossed the Sahara and traveled to West Africa with salt and other goods, returning to North Africa with gold.

- The empire of Ghana rose in the 300s. The empire grew rich by controlling the gold–salt trade. It was at the height of its power by the 800s.

- The empire of Mali controlled the gold–salt trade from the 1200s to the early 1500s. Its most famous king Mansa Musa caught the attention of the Islamic world when he traveled to Mecca on pilgrimage, impressing everyone with his vast supplies of gold and other riches.

- The empire of Songhai was the largest of the West African empires but also the shortest lived. It extended over most of the Sahel in West Africa but only existed for a little over 100 years from the mid-1400s to the late 1500s.

Why Does It Matter?

Sophisticated empires rose in West Africa by taking advantage of trade routes between gold and salt mines. In many ways, these empires were more developed than cultures in Western Europe at the time.

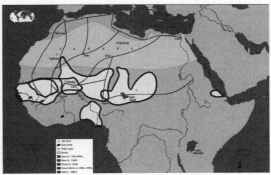

photo: Discovery Education

This map shows the location of the major West African empires.

2 Trading Kingdoms

Other kingdoms developed in Africa based on trade. Some traded in gold, others in rare goods such as ivory and leopard skins. Most participated in the slave trade as well.

- The West African Kingdom of Benin developed as a trading and cultural center at the mouth of the Niger River. Trade with Europeans allowed the kingdon to gain power over neighboring people in the interior.

- The kingdom of Aksum on the Red Sea used trade with the Arabian Peninsula to gain power and wealth. At the height of its power, the kingdom of Aksum controlled much of what is now modern-day Eritrea and Ethiopia as well as what is now Yemen on the Arabian peninsula.

- City-states along the coast of East Africa participated in trade with other civilizations in the Indian Ocean basin, such as Persia and India.

- Merchants took advantage of the seasonal monsoon winds and used ships called dhows to travel the long distances across the ocean.

- The Swahili culture became a mixture of African and Arab culture as a result of continual contact with Arab traders.

- The city of Great Zimbabwe controlled the gold trade between gold mines in southern Africa and the city-states on the Indian Ocean coast.

- The people of Great Zimbabwe constructed an enormous stone city, which is the oldest structure of its kind in Sub-Saharan Africa.

Why Does It Matter?

African empires built on trade both influenced and were influenced by their trading partners. These empires were involved in an intricate web of trade that connected them with other civilizations around the world.

photo: Bigstock

This stele is in the ancient city of Aksum.

Name _____ **Date** _____

 GRAPHIC ORGANIZER: Comparison Chart

Use this Comparison Chart to compare and contrast African empires. For supporting resources, go to Power and Change in Asia, Africa, and the Americas > African Empires > Growth of African Empires > Explore > Empires Rise.

African Empire	Characteristics	Effects of Trade on the Empire
Ghana		
Mali		
Songhai		
Kanem-Bornu		

Name _____ Date _____

GRAPHIC ORGANIZER: Comparison Chart *(continued)*

African Empire	Characteristics	Effects of Trade on the Empire
Benin		
Aksum		
Swahili City-States		
Great Zimbabwe		

Name _____ Date _____

EXPLORE: FOCUS QUESTIONS

Using what you learned from the Core Interactive Text, answer each page's focus question:

Salt and Gold

How did trade affect the rise of empires in West Africa?

_____
_____
_____

Empires Rise

How did the West African empires gain power?

_____
_____
_____

The Mali Empire

Who was Mansa Musa?

_____
_____
_____

The Songhai Empire

How did the Songhai Empire gain power?

_____
_____
_____

Kanem-Bornu

How did Kanem-Bornu gain power?

_____
_____
_____

Name _____ Date _____

EXPLORE: FOCUS QUESTIONS *(continued)*

The Kingdom of Benin
How was the Kingdom of Benin affected by its trade with the Portuguese?

_____

_____

_____

The Aksum Kingdom
What helped trading centers to develop along the coast of the Indian Ocean in Africa?

_____

_____

_____

Swahili Traders
How did Swahili traders contribute to a blending of cultures?

_____

_____

_____

Great Zimbabwe
What made Great Zimbabwe rich?

_____

_____

_____

PROJECTS AND ASSESSMENTS

Explain Activities

ACTIVITY TYPE: DIAGRAM

Trade and African Empires

In this activity, you will use at least eight words from the word bank to create a graphic answer to the following questions: What groups and resources were involved in trade in Africa? How did geography affect trade?

ACTIVITY TYPE: QUICK WRITE

Trade and African Life

In this Quick Write, you will compare and contrast the effects of trade on one of the major western empires in Africa to one of the smaller central and eastern empires in Africa.

ACTIVITY TYPE: SOCIAL STUDIES EXPLANATION

Growth of African Empires

In this Social Studies Explanation activity, you will use a template to assemble evidence from the sources you have explored. Then, you will write an answer to the Essential Question and defend your answer with supporting evidence.

Elaborate Activities

photo: Getty Images

INVESTIGATION TYPE: TIMELINE MAP

Built on Salt and Gold

How did trade influence the rise and fall of three major West African empires? In this investigation, you will use the Timeline Map and text to examine the rise and fall of the Mali, Ghana, and Songhai empires. Then, you will explain how each of these empires was influenced by the trading of salt, gold, and other precious metals.

photo: Pixabay

ACTIVITY TYPE: CURRENT EVENTS CONNECTION

Importance of Trans-Saharan Trade

In this activity, you will prepare a written essay or a speech that compares and contrasts the importance of trans-Saharan trade during the period of the African empires with modern trade in those areas and the effects on African society.

PROJECTS AND ASSESSMENTS *(continued)*

photo: Pixabay

ACTIVITY TYPE: ROLE PLAY

Timbuktu in the 1500s

In this activity, you will imagine you are a trader who comes to Timbuktu for the first time. Write a journal entry that describes your experiences and the people and things that are new and different to you.

photo: IRC

ACTIVITY TYPE: DOCUMENT-BASED INVESTIGATION

The Effects of Trade on African Empires

In this activity, you will either write the introduction to the presentation of a documentary or write a speech to present at a fair detailing the ways in which trade influenced the culture of early African empires.

Evaluate Activities

BRIEF-CONSTRUCTED RESPONSE (BCR)

Trade in East and West Africa

EXTENDED-CONSTRUCTED RESPONSE (ECR)

Trade in East and West Africa

UNIT 2: POWER AND CHANGE IN ASIA, AFRICA, AND THE AMERICAS

Chapter 8: African Empires

8.3 Religion and Culture in Africa

photo: Getty Images

LESSON OVERVIEW

Lesson Objectives:

By the end of this lesson, you should be able to:

- Describe the indigenous religions practiced in Africa before the introduction of Christianity and Islam.
- Trace the influences of Islam and Christianity on African cultures.

Key Vocabulary

Aksum, Coptic Christianity, indigenous, King Ezana, Mali Empire, Mansa Musa, Mecca, monotheism, Muhammad, polytheism, Timbuktu

Lesson Essential Question:

How did contact with other religions change life in Africa?

FLASHCARDS

1 Traditional Religion in Africa

For thousands of years, the natives of Africa have practiced traditional religions.

- Most traditional religions are indigenous to Africa.
- The traditional religions of Africa have many differences but also have overarching similarities.
- The traditional religions of Africa are polytheistic.
- The traditional religions all recognize the existence of a supreme god.
- Most of the followers of Africa's traditional religions seek guidance and help from lesser gods and dead ancestors.
- Followers believe their ancestors act as mediators between the physical world and the spiritual world.
- Africa's traditional religions have mostly remained active in the specific region of the ethnic group that practices them.

Why Does It Matter?

Traditional religions continue to be practiced by many people throughout Africa today. Also, the Christian and Muslim churches in Africa often mix in some of the beliefs and rituals of the traditional religions.

photo: Bigstock

Members of the Masai ethnic group in Africa perform a traditional dance that involves jumping for a ceremony.

2 Christianity and Islam Influence African Culture

Christianity entered Egypt before 100, and Islam began to spread through northern Africa during the 600s.

- Christians in Egypt formed the Coptic Church.
- During the early 300s, many people in Aksum began to convert to Christianity.
- Ezana, the king of Aksum, converted to Christianity around 321 and made it the state religion.
- The Aksumites continued to practice Christianity, despite being surrounded by Muslim-controlled territory.
- During the 600s, Muslim Arabs conquered North Africa and made this region part of the Muslim caliphate.
- The Muslims set up a class structure in the areas they conquered.
- The Muslims made a large cultural impact on North Africa, especially in the areas of math, science, literature, and architecture.
- During the 800s, Muslim merchants from North Africa began to convert people in West Africa.
- Mansa Musa made a pilgrimage to Mecca that involved thousands of followers and camels loaded with gold.
- The pilgrimage of Mansa Musa spread news of the great wealth of Mali and, as a result, many countries wanted to find the source of this wealth.

Why Does It Matter?

Christianity continues to be practiced in Ethiopia (formerly Aksum). Also, after establishing pockets of control along the African coast, European powers moved inland and took control of most of Africa during the 1800s. During this time, a large number of Christian missionaries entered Africa and converted many natives. Despite this fact, Islam remains the dominant religion in many African countries.

photo: Bigstock

This obelisk was created in Aksum for King Ezana. An obelisk is a stone pillar that tapers toward the top. The Aksumites constructed many obelisks and used them to announce important events.

Name _____ **Date** _____

 GRAPHIC ORGANIZER: Main Idea Web

Use this Main Idea Web to record characteristics of traditional religions in Africa. For supporting resources, go to Power and Change in Asia, Africa, and the Americas > African Empires > Religion and Culture in Africa > Explore > Traditional Religion in Africa.

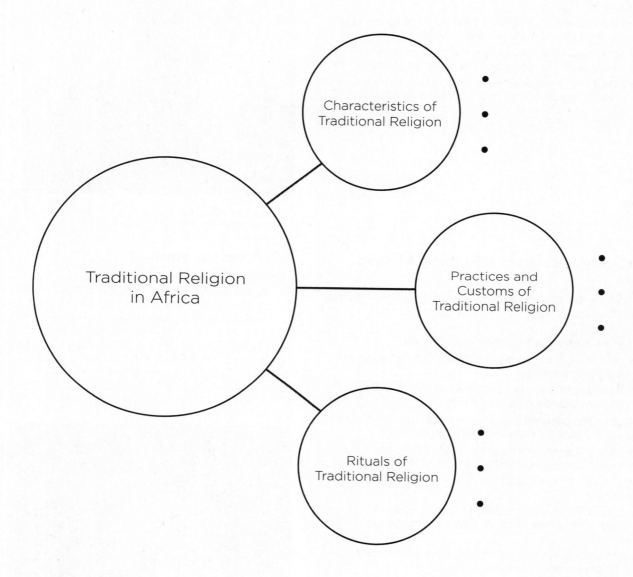

© Discovery Education | www.DiscoveryEducation.com

Name _____ **Date** _____

GRAPHIC ORGANIZER: Sequencing Chart

Complete this Sequencing Chart by listing in chronological order events in the establishment of Christianity in Africa. For supporting resources, go to Power and Change in Asia, Africa, and the Americas > African Empires > Religion and Culture in Africa > Explore > Christianity Enters Africa.

Event	Date	Summary	Significance

SOCIAL STUDIES
TECHBOOK

Name _____ Date _____

GRAPHIC ORGANIZER: Summary Frames

Use these Summary Frames to depict and describe events leading to the spread of Islam in Africa. For supporting resources, go to Power and Change in Asia, Africa, and the Americas > African Empires > Religion and Culture in Africa > Explore > Islam Spreads to Africa.

Name _____ **Date** _____

EXPLORE: FOCUS QUESTIONS

Using what you learned from the Core Interactive Text, answer each page's focus question:

Traditional Religion in Africa

What was traditional religion in Africa like?

_____

_____

_____

Talking to the Gods

What practices and customs do traditional African religions use to communicate with the gods?

_____

_____

_____

The Importance of Ceremonies and Ancestors

What are some of the rituals of traditional African religions?

_____

_____

_____

Christianity Enters Africa

What type of Christianity formed in Africa?

_____

_____

_____

Christianity Spreads to Aksum

How did Christianity spread to the kingdom of Aksum and other parts of Africa?

_____

_____

_____

Name _____ Date _____

EXPLORE: FOCUS QUESTIONS *(continued)*

Islam Spreads to Africa
How did Islam impact North Africa?

_____
_____
_____

Mansa Musa
How did Mansa Musa impact Africa and other regions?

_____
_____
_____

© Discovery Education | www.DiscoveryEducation.com

PROJECTS AND ASSESSMENTS

Explain Activities

ACTIVITY TYPE: DIAGRAM

Religion and Culture in Africa

In this 3-Way Venn Diagram activity, you will compare and contrast the spread of Christianity and Islam in Africa. Before you complete the 3-Way Venn Diagram, use the chart to list various characteristics about the spread of Christianity and Islam in Africa.

ACTIVITY TYPE: QUICK WRITE

Religion and Culture in Africa

In this Quick Write, you will take the perspective of a researcher who is studying the traditional religions of Africa for a book that will compare the shared features of these religions.

ACTIVITY TYPE: SOCIAL STUDIES EXPLANATION

Religion and Culture in Africa

In this Social Studies Explanation activity, you will use a template to assemble evidence from the sources you have explored. Then, you will write an answer to the Essential Question and defend your answer with supporting evidence.

Elaborate Activities

photo: Getty Images

INVESTIGATION TYPE: SOURCE ANALYSIS

Trade Kingdoms in West Africa

How did trade impact the development of African civilizations? Your mission is to analyze trade networks throughout Africa and draw conclusions about the spread of wealth and ideas.

PROJECTS AND ASSESSMENTS *(continued)*

photo: Getty Images

ACTIVITY TYPE: EXPRESS YOUR OPINION

Influences on Christian Art in Northeast Africa

In this activity, you will compare and contrast the pre-Christian art and architecture of northeast Africa, the art and architecture of this region after Christianity arrived, and the Christian art and architecture in other parts of the world. Then you will create a museum exhibit, documentary, or slideshow on whether the art and architecture had more in common with Christian art around the world or local art.

photo: Getty Images

ACTIVITY TYPE: ROLE PLAY

Interviewing Muslims in West Africa

For this activity, you will play the role of a person living during the Mali Empire and be interviewed by other students. You will also interview students playing the other roles and record their answers. Then, you will summarize the activity by discussing the effects of the arrival of Islam in West Africa.

photo: Getty Images

ACTIVITY TYPE: DOCUMENT-BASED INVESTIGATION

Life After the Arrival of Islam in West Africa

In this activity, you will write a report to a historical society that explains how the arrival of Islam impacted the lives of the people in West Africa. Or, you can create a slideshow using images and text to present at a conference that showcases how Islam impacted the lives of the people.

PROJECTS AND ASSESSMENTS *(continued)*

Evaluate Activities

BRIEF-CONSTRUCTED RESPONSE (BCR)

Religion and Culture in Africa

EXTENDED-CONSTRUCTED RESPONSE (ECR)

Religion and Culture in Africa

UNIT 3: NEW HORIZONS, NEW IDEAS

Chapter 9: The Renaissance

9.1 The Renaissance: Origins and Characteristics

photo: Getty Images

LESSON OVERVIEW

Lesson Objectives:

By the end of this lesson, you should be able to:

- **Define Renaissance and discuss its impact on society.**
- **Trace the origins and growth of the Renaissance from Italy throughout Europe.**

Lesson Essential Question:

How did global contact create social and cultural change during the Renaissance?

Key Vocabulary

China, Christianity, city-state, England, Europe, Florence, France, goods, Greece, Holy Roman Empire, humanism, Johannes Gutenberg, Mediterranean Sea, merchant, Michelangelo, Middle Ages, Muslims, Petrarch, Renaissance, republic, republicanism, Rome, Sir Thomas More, Spain, trade

FLASHCARDS

1 ## The Characteristics of the Renaissance

During the 1300s, some scholars changed the way they viewed the world, which led to the Renaissance.

- During the Middle Ages, people viewed life as a series of sufferings and temptations that must be endured and resisted to reach heaven after death.
- Humanists refocused religion and other learning on helping the living and improving life—a change in thinking that led to the Renaissance.
- Humanists realized that the teachings of the ancient Greeks and Romans could be applied to the concerns of everyday life.
- Humanists began to make advances in many areas, including science, art, architecture, and literature.
- Humanists emphasized the importance of free inquiry and criticism.
- Humanist thinkers found the works of classical writers in monastery libraries and prepared new editions of these works and translated them.
- Petrarch and other humanists thought that aspects of the ancient Greek and Roman civilizations, such as the arts, sciences, and government, could serve as models for their societies.
- Humanists viewed cities as places where people could use civic virtues, such as justice.

Why Does It Matter?

The shift in thinking from seeing life as a series of sufferings to be endured to wanting to improve life is a change that still affects our daily lives. Most cultures in the world today value trying to help people and improving life. As a result, great advances have been made in science, medicine, and technology.

photo: National Gallery of Art

Pietro Bembo was a Humanist scholar.

FLASHCARDS *(continued)*

2 ▶ The Origins and Growth of the Renaissance

The Renaissance began in Italy and spread throughout Europe.

- During the Middle Ages, city-states, instead of fiefs, developed in Italy.
- Many city-states, such as Venice, became very wealthy because of trade.
- The leaders of the city-states used their wealth to support Renaissance artists and scholars, and as a result, the Renaissance began to flourish in Italy.
- Ideas from nations in the Middle East and Asia spread to Italy through the trade routes Italian city-states had established.
- Two forms of government dominated the Italian city-states: the signoria and republicanism.
- During the late 1400s, the Renaissance began to spread to other areas of Europe.
- Merchants, diplomats, and scholars who visited Italy and soldiers who invaded Italy were inspired by Renaissance art and learning. When they returned home, they spread this knowledge.
- Monarchs of England, France, and Spain adopted the culture of Renaissance Italy in their countries and also supported Renaissance artists from their countries.
- The invention of the printing press greatly increased the number of books produced and thereby helped to spread Renaissance ideas.
- In northern Europe, scholars developed Christian humanism, which attempted to reform the Catholic Church.

Why Does It Matter?

The spread of humanist ideas changed the arts and learning throughout Europe and formed the basis for Western culture. Also, these ideas would inspire other movements, such as the Reformation, the Age of Exploration, and the Scientific Revolution.

photo: Library of Congress

During the Renaissance, the Erbaria served as a wholesale market for merchants dealing in produce. Commerce brought great wealth to Italian city-states. This wealth was often used to support Renaissance artists and scholars.

Name _____ **Date** _____

GRAPHIC ORGANIZER: Venn Diagram

Use this Venn Diagram to compare and contrast the two forms of government in Italian city-states: the signoria and republicanism. For supporting resources, go to New Horizons, New Ideas > The Renaissance > The Renaissance: Origins and Characteristics > Explore > The Governments of Italian City-States.

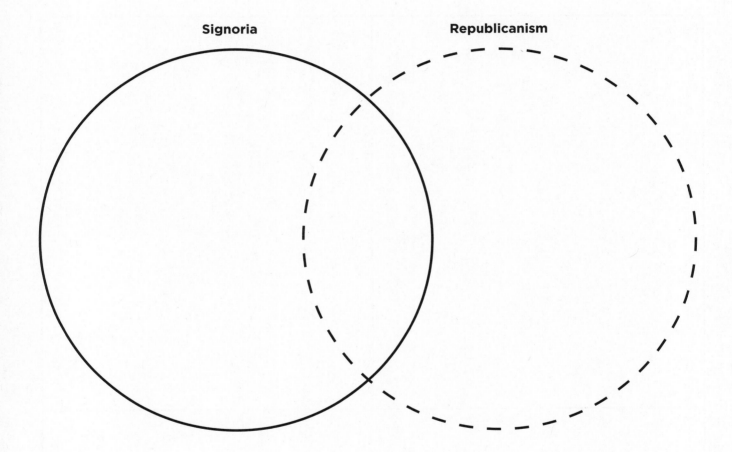

Signoria   **Republicanism**

Name _____ **Date** _____

GRAPHIC ORGANIZER: Change Over Time Chart

Use this Change Over Time Chart to analyze the changes brought about by the Renaissance. In the "Before" column, record characteristics of Europe during the Middle Ages. In the "After" column, record characteristics of Europe during the Renaissance. Then, in the space provided at the bottom of the chart, summarize the changes that took place in Europe from the Middle Ages through the Renaissance era. For supporting resources, go to New Horizons, New Ideas > The Renaissance > The Renaissance: Origins and Characteristics > Explore > A Shift in Thinking.

Before:

After:

Changes:

Name _____ **Date** _____

GRAPHIC ORGANIZER: Summary Frames

Use these Summary Frames to illustrate and describe six important events in the development of the Renaissance in Italy. For supporting resources, go to New Horizons, New Ideas > The Renaissance > The Renaissance: Origins and Characteristics > Explore > The Birthplace of the Renaissance.

Name _____ Date _____

 GRAPHIC ORGANIZER: Influences and Effects Graphic Organizer

Use this Influences and Effects graphic organizer to analyze the ways in which other cultures influenced the Renaissance movement in Italy and to describe how ideas central to this movement spread beyond Italy, having an effect on other areas of Europe. For supporting resources, go to New Horizons, New Ideas > The Renaissance > The Renaissance: Origins and Characteristics > Explore > Muslims and Other Peoples Influence the Renaissance.

How Did Other Cultures Influence Italy?

Muslim Mathematics:	Muslim Science:	Chinese Influence:
•	•	•
•	•	•
•	•	•

Renaissance Italy

How Did Ideas Spread Beyond Italy?

Name _____ **Date** _____

GRAPHIC ORGANIZER: Summary Frames

Complete these Summary Frames by illustrating and describing the factors that led to the spread of Renaissance ideas. For supporting resources, go to New Horizons, New Ideas > The Renaissance > The Renaissance: Origins and Characteristics > Explore > The Renaissance Spreads Beyond Italy.

_____   _____   _____

_____   _____   _____

_____   _____   _____

_____   _____   _____

_____   _____   _____

_____   _____   _____

Name _____ Date _____

EXPLORE: FOCUS QUESTIONS

Using what you learned from the Core Interactive Text, answer each page's focus question:

The Governments of Italian City-States
What types of governments did the Italian city-states have?

_____
_____
_____

A Shift in Thinking
How did a change in thinking lead to the development of the Renaissance?

_____
_____
_____

The Development of Humanism
How did humanism develop?

_____
_____
_____

The Birthplace of the Renaissance
Why did the Renaissance begin in Italy?

_____
_____
_____

Muslims and Other Peoples Influence the Renaissance
How did ideas from regions outside of Europe influence the Renaissance?

_____
_____
_____

Name _____ Date _____

EXPLORE: FOCUS QUESTIONS *(continued)*

The Renaissance Spreads Beyond Italy
How did the Renaissance spread throughout Europe?

_____

_____

_____

A Growing Idea
How did the ideas of the Renaissance continue to spread and grow?

_____

_____

_____

PROJECTS AND ASSESSMENTS

Explain Activities

ACTIVITY TYPE: DIAGRAM

Renaissance: Origins and Characteristics

In this activity, you will use a word bank to create a graphic response to the Essential Question.

ACTIVITY TYPE: YOU AS JOURNALIST

Renaissance: Origins and Characteristics

In this activity, you will write an article from the point of view of a Northern European identifying new ideas and innovations from Italy that are influencing your society.

ACTIVITY TYPE: SOCIAL STUDIES EXPLANATION

The Renaissance: Origins and Characteristics

In this Social Studies Explanation activity, you will use a template to assemble evidence from the sources you have explored. Then, you will write an answer to the Essential Question and defend your answer with supporting evidence.

Elaborate Activities

photo: Getty Images

INVESTIGATION TYPE: MAP-GUIDED INQUIRY

From Darkness to Light: A Tour of Renaissance Europe

How did the Renaissance change Europe?

photo: Getty Images

ACTIVITY TYPE: SAY WHAT?

Humanism and Religion

In this activity, you will create an article or a collage of words that describes what Renaissance thinkers believed was needed to lead a religious life.

PROJECTS AND ASSESSMENTS *(continued)*

photo: Getty Images

ACTIVITY TYPE: ROLE PLAY

Italian City-States

In this activity, you will compare and contrast an Italian city-state during the Middle Ages and the Renaissance by either writing a diary entry or drawing two pictures. You will use historical evidence to support your final product.

photo: Getty Images

ACTIVITY TYPE: DOCUMENT-BASED INVESTIGATION

Origins of the Renaissance

In this Document-Based Investigation, you will analyze the sources and investigate this question: What ideas and innovations helped create the Renaissance?

Evaluate Activities

BRIEF-CONSTRUCTED RESPONSE (BCR)

Renaissance: Origins and Characteristics

EXTENDED-CONSTRUCTED RESPONSE (ECR)

Renaissance: Origins and Characteristics

UNIT 3: NEW HORIZONS, NEW IDEAS

Chapter 9: The Renaissance

9.2 Renaissance Cultural Contributions

photo: Getty Images

LESSON OVERVIEW

Lesson Objectives:

By the end of this lesson, you should be able to:

- **Identify important Renaissance figures (Machiavelli, Leonardo da Vinci, Shakespeare, and Gutenberg) and developments.**

- **Analyze the impact of these developments on European society.**

Lesson Essential Question:

How did innovations of the Renaissance influence the development of Western society?

Key Vocabulary

Age of Exploration, Andreas Vesalius, circumnavigate, city-state, England, Europe, Florence, France, humanism, Italy, Ivan the Terrible, Jan van Eyck, Johannes Gutenberg, Johannes Kepler, King John of England, Leonardo da Vinci, Machiavelli, Nicolaus Copernicus, Raphael, Renaissance, Spain, William Shakespeare

FLASHCARDS

1 Renaissance Art and Literature

Renaissance thinkers produced works of art, literature, and philosophy that are still important today.

- Renaissance thinkers were interested in the human experience. They believed humans could do anything, and examined ways to achieve perfection.
- Niccoló Machiavelli wrote a treatise on what it takes to be a perfect leader. A key point in his book *The Prince* is that "the end justifies the means."
- Leonardo da Vinci was an all-around Renaissance man. A painter, inventor, engineer, and sculptor, he drew ideas for many inventions that would not be possible for years to come, like the airplane.
- Da Vinci painted the *Mona Lisa*, one of the most famous paintings in the world to date.
- William Shakespeare was a playwright and poet. He wrote *Romeo and Juliet, Hamlet*, and 35 other plays. He also wrote 154 sonnets.
- Shakespeare explored many themes about the human experience including love and revenge. His plays are still performed today, and many modern stories have been based on his ideas.
- Johannes Gutenberg invented the printing press. This machine allowed books to be easily produced for less money and less time than with the old-fashioned hand-copying methods used during the Middle Ages.
- With the printing press, ideas and information could be spread easily as books and pamphlets could be produced quickly and cheaply.

Why Does It Matter?

These important Renaissance figures all created something of lasting impact. Machiavelli changed how we look at politics and politicians, Shakespeare made theater important again and created a new form of poetry, and Gutenberg developed a machine that could be used to mass-produce literature quickly and cheaply. This meant that ideas could be spread throughout Europe relatively easily.

photo: Los Angeles County Museum of Art (www.lacma.org)
Da Vinci is often viewed as a perfect example of the ideal Renaissance man.

2 Science and Exploration

During the Renaissance, curious thinkers and explorers conducted research, experiments, and explorations to learn more about the human body and our world.

- Andreas Vesalius wrote an important book on anatomy. Published in 1543, *De Humani Corporis Fabrica* was the first accurate information on the human body.
- Vesalius conducted his research for the book by dissecting and studying human bodies.
- The Renaissance innovations also inspired the Age of Exploration. During this time period, European explorers looked for and found sea routes to Asia and beyond.

Why Does It Matter?

During the Age of Exploration, European explorers sailed around the world, learning of lands and new cultures and bringing European ideas outside of Europe. This exploration laid the groundwork for accurate maps and colonization of new lands. Meanwhile, the important discoveries being made by scientific minds like Andreas Vesalius's forever changed medicine.

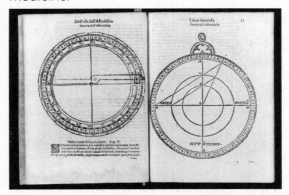

photo: Library of Congress
Navigational tools like the cross staff, astrolabe, and compass helped Renaissance sailors find their way in the open seas.

Name _____ **Date** _____

GRAPHIC ORGANIZER: Comparison Chart

Use this Comparison Chart to compare various aspects of important Renaissance figures. For supporting resources, go to New Horizons, New Ideas > The Renaissance > Renaissance Cultural Contributions > Explore > The Art of Politics.

Criteria	Location of Key Figure	Figure's Contribution to the Renaissance	Overall Significance of These Contributions
Niccoló Machiavelli			
Leonardo da Vinci			
Michelangelo			

Name _____ Date _____

GRAPHIC ORGANIZER: Comparison Chart *(continued)*

Criteria	Location of Key Figure	Figure's Contribution to the Renaissance	Overall Significance of These Contributions
Raphael			
Jan van Eyck			
William Shakespeare			

Name _____ Date _____

GRAPHIC ORGANIZER: Main Idea Web

Use this Main Idea Web to describe how the invention of the printing press, the works of Andreas Vesalius, and the discoveries made during the Age of Exploration contributed to the enduring influence of the Renaissance period. For supporting resources, go to New Horizons, New Ideas > The Renaissance > Renaissance Cultural Contributions > Explore > Spreading the Word.

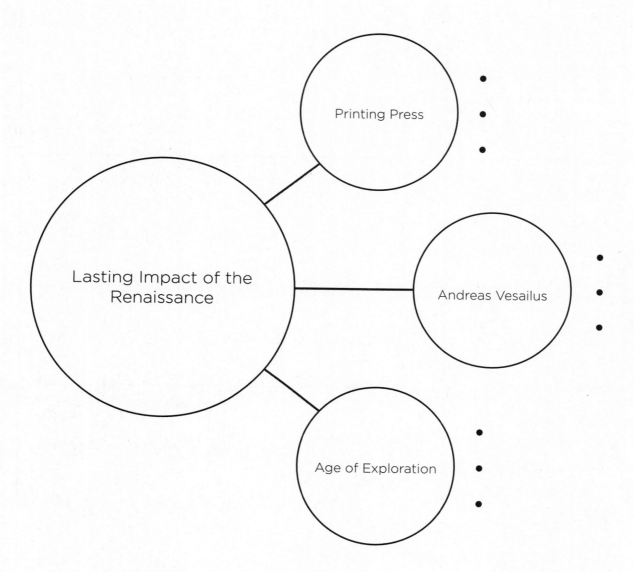

Name _____ Date _____

EXPLORE: FOCUS QUESTIONS

Using what you learned from the Core Interactive Text, answer each page's focus question:

The Art of Politics

What is the importance of Niccoló Machiavelli's book *The Prince*?

_____

_____

_____

A True Renaissance Man

Who was Leonardo da Vinci?

_____

_____

_____

Renaissance Artists

What other artists made significant contributions to Renaissance art?

_____

_____

_____

The Bard of Avon

What is the legacy of William Shakespeare?

_____

_____

_____

Spreading the Word

How did the invention of the printing press impact culture in the Renaissance?

_____

_____

_____

Name _____ **Date** _____

EXPLORE: FOCUS QUESTIONS *(continued)*

The Fabric of the Human Body
How did Andreas Vesalius change our understanding of the human body?

_____
_____
_____

Exploration and Discovery
How is the Renaissance related to the "Age of Exploration"?

_____
_____
_____

PROJECTS AND ASSESSMENTS

Explain Activities

ACTIVITY TYPE: ADVERTISEMENT

Renaissance Cultural Contributions

In this activity, you will create an advertisement for a specific product, innovation, or idea from the Renaissance.

ACTIVITY TYPE: YOU AS JOURNALIST

Renaissance Cultural Contributions

In this activity, you will write a short article about the contributions and developments made by some of the people living during the Renaissance period—and the impact that these contributions and developments have had on society, both past and present.

ACTIVITY TYPE: SOCIAL STUDIES EXPLANATION

Renaissance Cultural Contributions

In this Social Studies Explanation activity, you will use a template to assemble evidence from the sources you have explored. Then, you will write an answer to the Essential Question and defend your answer with supporting evidence.

Elaborate Activities

photo: IRC

INVESTIGATION TYPE: SOURCE ANALYSIS

The Renaissance Man

How do Leonardo da Vinci's sketchbooks represent the Renaissance? In this investigation, you will use the Source Analysis tool to examine some of da Vinci's sketches and notes and explain why he is considered a true Renaissance man.

ACTIVITY TYPE: PITCH YOUR IDEA

Bringing Leonardo's Designs to Life

In this activity, you will make plans to develop one of the contraptions, but first you will need funding and support from the Renaissance leaders of the time. To show Renaissance leaders the benefits of Leonardo's invention, you will create a proposal for building the invention and present your plan to the Renaissance leaders.

photo: Corbis

PROJECTS AND ASSESSMENTS *(continued)*

photo: Getty Images

ACTIVITY TYPE: CURRENT EVENTS CONNECTION

The Prince!

In this activity, you will research to learn more about Machiavelli's ideas and apply them to modern leaders. As the host of a modern reality show titled "The Prince!," you will judge several contemporary world leaders and award one the title of "The Prince."

photo: Getty Images

ACTIVITY TYPE: DOCUMENT-BASED INVESTIGATION

Renaissance Cultural Contributions

In this Document-Based Investigation, you will analyze source materials and investigate this question: How did humanist ideas change Europe?

Evaluate Activities

BRIEF-CONSTRUCTED RESPONSE (BCR)

Renaissance Cultural Contributions

EXTENDED-CONSTRUCTED RESPONSE (ECR)

Renaissance Cultural Contributions

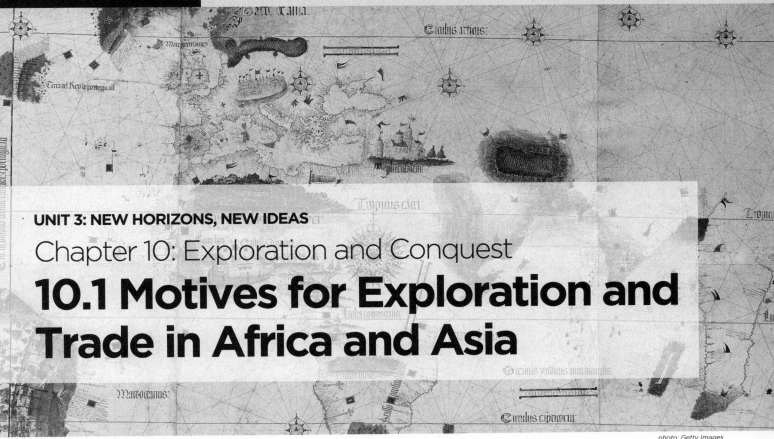

10.1 Motives for Exploration and Trade in Africa and Asia

photo: Getty Images

LESSON OVERVIEW

Lesson Objectives:

By the end of this lesson, you should be able to:

- **Analyze the motives for exploration and conquest by European nations.**
- **Trace the Age of Exploration and its effect on Africa.**
- **Explain the impact of the transatlantic slave trade on the African people.**
- **Trace the Age of Exploration and its effect on Asia.**

Lesson Essential Questions:

Why did European leaders want to explore and conquer? What was the impact of these encounters on other regions?

Key Vocabulary

Africa, Age of Exploration, Asia, astrolabe, barter, Bartolomeu Dias, Cape Town, caravel, China, Christianity, colony, compass, Congo River, Dutch East India Company, England, Europe, Ferdinand Magellan, France, Gobi Desert, goods, Great Britain, Hernando de Soto, Hernán Cortés, Hundred Years' War, Ibn Battuta, India, Jacques Cartier, Japan, Johannes Gutenberg, John Cabot, line of demarcation, Marco Polo, merchant, Middle East, missionary, Muslims, pirates, plantation, Prince Henry the Navigator, proselytizing religion / universalizing religion, Ptolemy, Samuel de Champlain, shogun, Silk Road, slavery, slaves, South America, Spain, Tokugawa Ieyasu, trade, Treaty of Tordesillas, Vasco da Gama, Vasco Núñez de Balboa

FLASHCARDS

1

Motives for European Exploration and Conquest

European explorers were primarily looking for a new trade route to Asia. However, some European rulers wanted to conquer new lands and spread Christianity.

- **Trade with Asia was restricted by the Muslim countries in the Middle East and Central Asia.**
- **Explorers looked for new sea routes to Asia to avoid traveling through Muslim countries.**
- **While looking for the new routes, explorers landed on the western coast of Africa.**
- **Prince Henry the Navigator developed a school for explorers to learn new techniques and build better ships.**
- **Better maps and new navigational tools, like the compass and quadrant, made longer voyages possible.**
- **Europeans were able to establish colonies in Africa, the West Indies, and North and South America.**
- **Missionaries traveled to colonies and trade stations to spread Christianity.**

Why Does It Matter?

The primary motivations behind European voyages of discovery were increased trade, profit, and Christian proselytizing. European nations used new technology to establish trade and colonies so they could increase their wealth and power. They also wanted to spread Christianity. European exploration led to the creation of colonies in Africa, the Americas, India, and Asia. These colonies led to an exchange in cultural ideas that greatly affected Europe and the cultures it came into contact with.

photo: Library of Congress

This European map from the late 1500s shows routes to the northern coast of Africa.

2

European Exploration and Africa

Portuguese explorers established European trade with Africa in the 1400s. In the 1600s, the Dutch established the first permanent European colony in Africa at Cape Town.

- **Prince Henry the Navigator directed expeditions that explored the western coast of Africa.**
- **Dias and da Gama sailed around the Cape of Good Hope, establishing a sea route to Asia. Da Gama also founded Portuguese colonies in East Africa.**
- **The African kingdoms traded gold, ivory, jewels, and exotic plants and animals in exchange for alcohol, gunpowder, and cowrie shells. The Africans also sold enslaved people.**
- **Eventually, Europeans were buying more enslaved people from the Africans than goods.**

Why Does It Matter?

Trade with Africa reduced European dependence on the Muslim nations that controlled trade with Asia. European nations and African coastal kingdoms both grew rich from the trade. European nations and their colonies soon became dependent on slave labor to run their plantations.

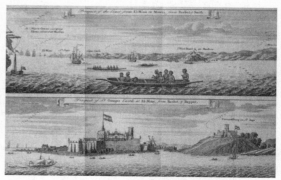

photo: From The New York Public Library

In West Africa, many European countries built "slave castles" off the coast as centers for the slave trade. This fort called El Mina, or Elmina, was originally built by the Portuguese in the 1400s, but it was operated by the Dutch until the 1800s.

FLASHCARDS *(continued)*

3 ### Impact of the Slave Trade on Africa

Selling enslaved Africans to Europeans enriched the coastal kingdoms but depleted Africa's population.

- European traders bought enslaved Africans to work in Europe and in the growing colonies in the West Indies and North and South America.
- African slave traders in the western coastal kingdoms grew wealthy selling enslaved people to Europeans.
- As European demand for enslaved Africans increased, slave hunters had to raid kingdoms that were farther inland.
- The most prized enslaved Africans were strong young men. This meant that many African kingdoms lost a great deal of their workforce.

Why Does It Matter?

The slave trade was a part of African culture before the Europeans arrived. However, the Europeans increased demand for enslaved Africans dramatically due to the growth of plantations in European colonies. This made the slave traders very wealthy, but it also depleted the workforce of the African kingdoms.

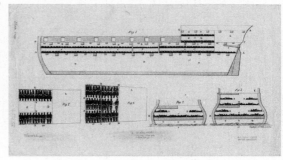

photo: From The New York Public Library
Enslaved Africans faced terrible conditions on ships across the Atlantic.

4 ### European Explorers and the East

European explorers established colonies and trading outposts in India, China, and Japan in the 1500s and 1600s.

- The Portuguese were the first European explorers to reach Asia by sea.
- Dutch traders took control of many African and Asian markets through the Dutch East India Company in the 1500s and 1600s.
- Indians were suspicious of the Europeans but eventually opened their coastal cities to trade.
- In the 1600s, the fall of the Mughal Empire in India made it possible for Great Britain to take control of trade from the French and Dutch colonists. Great Britain would maintain political control in India for a long time.
- China and Japan treated European traders with caution. Japan would eventually close its doors to Europe until the middle of the 1800s.
- Jesuit missionaries were welcomed in China but did not have much influence there. Christianity was initially embraced by the Japanese, but then it was outlawed.

Why Does It Matter?

Establishing direct trade with India and China allowed Europeans to avoid the Muslims who controlled trade along the Silk Road. This increased the wealth and power of the European nations. It also led to wars among Spain and Portugal, the Dutch Empire, England, and France as each tried to gain more power in the new markets. Contact with European traders and colonists had a significant cultural impact on India and China.

photo: From The New York Public Library
This European-style church was built in Southern India in 1830.

Name _____ **Date** _____

GRAPHIC ORGANIZER: GREASES Chart

Complete this GREASES Chart by identifying some of the reasons why the Europeans began their explorations in Africa and Asia. For supporting resources, go to New Horizons, New Ideas > Exploration and Conquest > Motives for Exploration and Trade in Africa and Asia > Explore > Seeking New Markets.

Government	
Religion	
Economic	
Art & Architecture	
Science & Technology	
Environment	
Social & Cultural Values	

Name _____ Date _____

GRAPHIC ORGANIZER: Problem/Solution Chart

Use this Problem/Solution Chart to record problems and solutions associated with each of the following categories: direction, latitude, longitude, and the printing press. For supporting resources, go to New Horizons, New Ideas > Exploration and Conquest > Motives for Exploration and Trade in Africa and Asia > Explore > Innovations in Navigation.

Problem   **Solution**

Direction

Latitude

Longitude

Printing Press

Name _____ Date _____

GRAPHIC ORGANIZER: Summary Frames

Complete these Summary Frames by describing the achievements of each of the Portuguese explorers. For supporting resources, go to New Horizons, New Ideas > Exploration and Conquest > Motives for Exploration and Trade in Africa and Asia > Explore > The Portuguese Expeditions.

Diogo Cam	Bartolomeu Dias	Vasco da Gama

_____   _____   _____

_____   _____   _____

_____   _____   _____

Name _____ Date _____

GRAPHIC ORGANIZER: Main Idea Web

Use this Main Idea Web to record information related to the African slave trade, including the reasons why the slave trade occurred and the far-reaching impact it had on people around the world. For supporting resources, go to New Horizons, New Ideas > Exploration and Conquest > Motives for Exploration and Trade in Africa and Asia > Explore > Ivory, Gold, and Enslaved Africans.

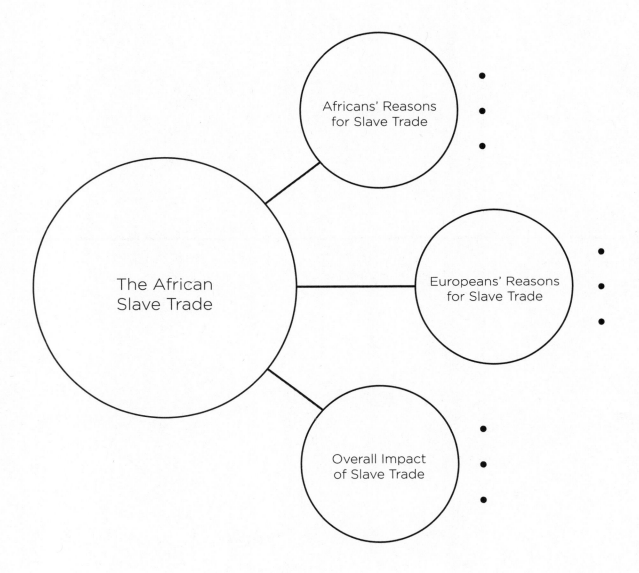

Name _____**Date** _____

GRAPHIC ORGANIZER: Timeline

Use this Timeline to trace the rise and fall of European powers in India and China from the 1400s to the 1700s. For supporting resources, go to New Horizons, New Ideas > Exploration and Conquest > Motives for Exploration and Trade in Africa and Asia > Explore > Trading with the East.

1400   1800

◆━━◆

Name _____ Date _____

EXPLORE: FOCUS QUESTIONS

Using what you learned from the Core Interactive Text, answer each page's focus question:

Seeking New Markets

What led to European exploration?

_____

_____

_____

Missionaries and Colonies

What role did Christianity play in European expansion to Africa?

_____

_____

_____

Innovations in Navigation

How did advances in sailing technology impact European exploration?

_____

_____

_____

A School for Sailors

What was Prince Henry's school?

_____

_____

_____

The Portuguese Expeditions

How did Europe first encounter Africa?

_____

_____

_____

Ivory, Gold, and Enslaved Africans

How did the African slave trade begin?

_____

_____

_____

Name _____**Date** _____

EXPLORE: FOCUS QUESTIONS *(continued)*

Impact of the Slave Trade
Where did enslaved Africans come from?

_____
_____
_____

Trading with the East
How did Europeans establish trade in Asia?

_____
_____
_____

Other Europeans Follow
How did trade increase between India, China, and the rest of the European nations?

_____
_____
_____

Europe and the East
How did China respond to European traders?

_____
_____
_____

Japan and the West
What was Japan's relationship with European traders?

_____
_____
_____

PROJECTS AND ASSESSMENTS

Explain Activities

ACTIVITY TYPE: ADVERTISEMENT

Motives for Exploration and Trade in Africa and Asia

In this activity, you will create an advertisement to persuade explorers to use a quadrant, an astrolabe, or a compass.

ACTIVITY TYPE: MOVIE TRAILER

Motives for Exploration and Trade in Africa and Asia

In this activity, you will create a movie trailer for a movie based on Diogo Cam's discovery of the Congo River, Bartolomeu Dias's trip around the Cape of Good Hope, Vasco da Gama's journey to India, Jan van Riebeeck's founding of Cape Town, or a Portuguese merchants' trip to the city of Canton in China.

ACTIVITY TYPE: SOCIAL STUDIES EXPLANATION

Motives for Exploration and Trade in Africa and Asia

In this Social Studies Explanation activity, you will use a template to assemble evidence from the sources you have explored. Then, you will write an answer to the Essential Question and defend your answer with supporting evidence.

Elaborate Activities

photo: Discovery Education

INVESTIGATION TYPE: HISTORICAL PERSPECTIVES

Motives for Exploration and Trade in Africa

Your mission is to get to know four individuals involved in the transatlantic slave trade. After reading their profiles, decide how each person might react to the key issues of the day.

photo: Getty's Open Content Program

ACTIVITY TYPE: ROLE PLAY

A European in Asia

In this activity, you will take on the role of a European trader in Asia in the 1500s and write about your reactions to life in Asia in either a journal entry or a letter to a friend.

PROJECTS AND ASSESSMENTS *(continued)*

photo: Getty Images

ACTIVITY TYPE: EXPRESS YOUR OPINION

To Trade or Not to Trade?
In this activity, you will prepare to give a speech to a West African tribal leader who is trying to decide whether to trade with European nations.

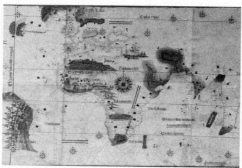

photo: Getty Images

ACTIVITY TYPE: DOCUMENT-BASED INVESTIGATION

Motives for Exploration and Trade in Africa
In this Document-Based Investigation, you will analyze source materials and investigate this question: What were European motives for exploring Africa during the Age of Exploration?

Evaluate Activities

BRIEF-CONSTRUCTED RESPONSE (BCR)

Motives for Exploration and Trade in Africa and Asia

EXTENDED-CONSTRUCTED RESPONSE (ECR)

Motives for Exploration and Trade in Africa and Asia

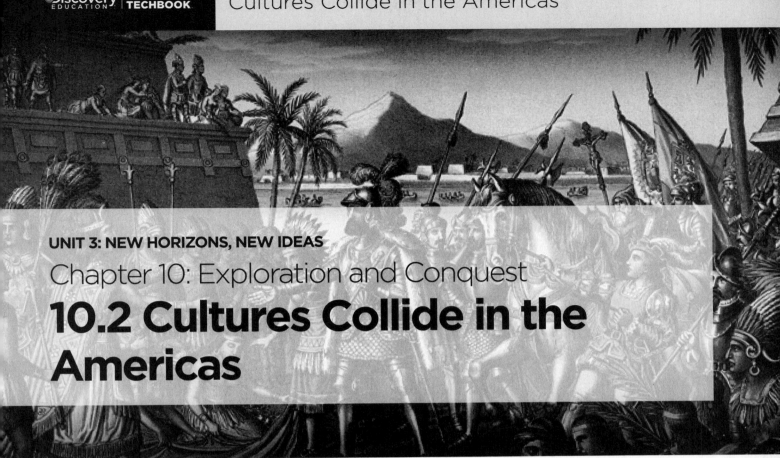

UNIT 3: NEW HORIZONS, NEW IDEAS

Chapter 10: Exploration and Conquest

10.2 Cultures Collide in the Americas

LESSON OVERVIEW

Lesson Objective:

By the end of this lesson, you should be able to:

- Analyze the causes and effects of European exploration of the Americas on the native people of the Americas and the economy of Europe.

Lesson Essential Question:

How did European contact and conquest in America change life in the Americas and in Europe?

Key Vocabulary

Africa, Amerigo Vespucci, Asia, Atahualpa, Atlantic Ocean, Aztec, Aztec Empire, caravel, China, Christianity, Christopher Columbus, colony, Columbian Exchange, conquistador, culture, encomienda, epidemic, Europe, expedition, Ferdinand Magellan, Francisco Pizarro, Giovanni da Verrazzano, Henry Hudson, Hernando de Soto, Hernán Cortés, Inca, Jacques Cartier, Japan, John Cabot, Juan Ponce de León, King Louis IV, line of demarcation, Mexico, mission, missionary, Montezuma, New Spain, Peru, population, Prince Henry the Navigator, Queen Isabella, Renaissance, Samuel de Champlain, South America, Spain, Tenochtitlán, trade, Treaty of Paris, Treaty of Tordesillas, Vasco da Gama, Vasco Núñez de Balboa

FLASHCARDS

1 Cultures Collide

During the first centuries following Columbus's voyage to the Americas, Europeans invaded the Native Americans' lands.

- Hernán Cortés and Francisco Pizarro were able to conquer the powerful Aztec and Inca empires easily because of European diseases and civil war that had ravaged the empires.

- Europeans viewed the Native Americans as a source of labor and as potential converts to Christianity. Some treated the Native Americans well, and others treated them very harshly. Limited actions were made to promote cultural understanding.

Why Does It Matter?

Early interactions between Europeans and Native Americans shaped and developed the growing population and culture in the Americas.

photo: Corbis

Pizarro's capture of Atahualpa allowed him to conquer and rule the Incan Empire.

2 The Columbian Exchange

The Columbian Exchange affected all areas of the world.

- The Columbian Exchange was the movement of plants, animals, and diseases between the Eastern and Western hemispheres.

- The Columbian Exchange had positive effects, such as the introduction of new foods to European and African cuisine and the introduction of new domesticated animals, such as the horse, to the New World.

- The Columbian Exchange also had negative effects, namely the spreading of new diseases among the Native Americans. European diseases killed large numbers of Native Americans, who did not have any resistance to the diseases.

Why Does It Matter?

The Columbian Exchange shaped history in both the Old World and the New World as goods from both hemispheres mixed. It changed economies, populations, cuisines, and cultures.

photo: Pixabay

The potato, green beans, squash, and maize (corn) were all unknown to Europeans before contact with the Americas.

Name _____**Date** _____

GRAPHIC ORGANIZER: Main Idea Web

Use this Main Idea Web to record the main motivations for European exploration. For supporting resources, go to New Horizons, New Ideas > Exploration and Conquest > Cultures Collide in the Americas > Explore > Reasons for Exploration.

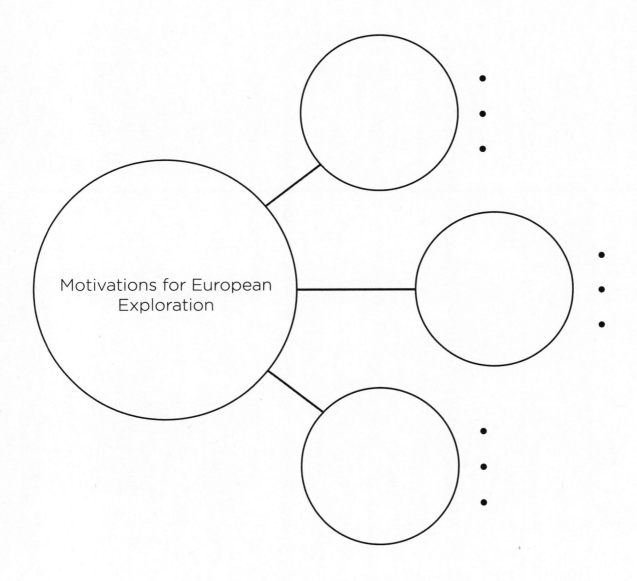

Name _____ **Date** _____

GRAPHIC ORGANIZER: Timeline

Use this Timeline to trace the important voyages and events in the exploration and conquest of the American continents. For supporting resources, go to New Horizons, New Ideas > Exploration and Conquest > Cultures Collide in the Americas > Explore > Europeans Arrive in the Caribbean.

1492   1700

◆———◆

Name _____**Date** _____

GRAPHIC ORGANIZER: Main Idea Web

Use this Main Idea Web to record the different resources and tools that helped the Spanish conquer native populations, and why each was important. For supporting resources, go to New Horizons, New Ideas > Exploration and Conquest > Cultures Collide in the Americas > Explore > Conquering the Americas.

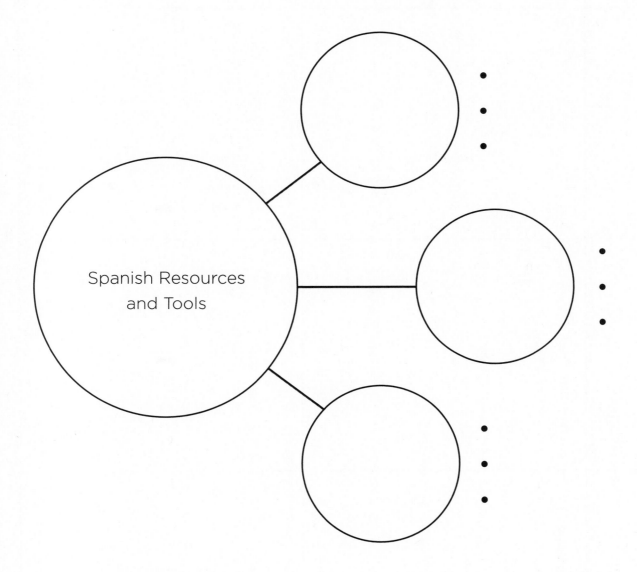

Name _____ **Date** _____

GRAPHIC ORGANIZER: Comparison Chart

Use this Comparison Chart to compare and contrast the conquests of the Aztec and the Inca. For supporting resources, go to New Horizons, New Ideas > Exploration and Conquest > Cultures Collide in the Americas > Explore > Cortés and the Aztec.

Criteria	Aztec	Inca
Who		
When		
Where		

Name _____**Date** _____

GRAPHIC ORGANIZER: Comparison Chart *(continued)*

Criteria	Aztec	Inca
Why		
How		

Name _____**Date** _____

GRAPHIC ORGANIZER: Comparison Chart

Use this Comparison Chart to compare and contrast the mission and encomienda systems. For supporting resources, go to New Horizons, New Ideas > Exploration and Conquest > Cultures Collide in the Americas > Explore > Missions and Missionaries.

Criteria	Missions	Encomiendas
General Description		
Purpose		

Name _____**Date** _____

GRAPHIC ORGANIZER: Comparison Chart *(continued)*

Criteria	Missions	Encomiendas
Effects on European Settlers		
Effects on Native Americans		

Name _____ **Date** _____

GRAPHIC ORGANIZER: Change Over Time Chart

Use this Change Over Time Chart to record the characteristics of life in Europe and the Americas before and after the Columbian Exchange. For supporting resources, go to New Horizons, New Ideas > Exploration and Conquest > Cultures Collide in the Americas > Explore > Tomatoes for Horses.

Europe Before the Exchange	Europe After the Exchange
The Americas Before the Exchange	**The Americas After the Exchange**

Overall Trends of These Changes:

© Discovery Education | www.DiscoveryEducation.com

Name _____ Date _____

EXPLORE: FOCUS QUESTIONS

Using what you learned from the Core Interactive Text, answer each page's focus question:

Reasons for Exploration
Why did Europeans first arrive in the Americas?

_____

_____

_____

Europeans Arrive in the Caribbean
What was Columbus's role in the exploration and colonization of the Caribbean and the American continents?

_____

_____

_____

Conquering the Americas
How were the Spanish able to conquer Native American populations?

_____

_____

_____

Cortés and the Aztec
How was Cortés able to conquer the Aztec Empire?

_____

_____

_____

Pizarro and the Inca
How was Pizarro able to conquer the Inca Empire?

_____

_____

_____

Name _____ Date _____

EXPLORE: FOCUS QUESTIONS *(continued)*

Missions and Missionaries
How did Spanish missionaries change life in the Americas?

_____
_____
_____
_____

Encomiendas
What was the encomienda system?

_____
_____
_____
_____

The English in the Americas
What were the first British colonies in the Americas?

_____
_____
_____
_____

The French and Dutch in the Americas
What areas of the Americas did the French and Dutch colonize?

_____
_____
_____
_____

Tomatoes for Horses
How did the Columbian Exchange change life in Europe and the Americas?

_____
_____
_____
_____

Clash of Empires
How did competition for land affect the relationships between empires?

_____
_____
_____
_____

PROJECTS AND ASSESSMENTS

Explain Activities

ACTIVITY TYPE: DIAGRAM

Cultures Collide in the Americas

In this activity, you will use a word bank to create a graphic answer to the Essential Question: How did European contact and conquest change life in the Americas and in Europe?

ACTIVITY TYPE: YOU AS JOURNALIST

Spanish Treatment of Native Americans

In this activity, you will write a newspaper article describing your visit to either a mission or an encomienda.

ACTIVITY TYPE: SOCIAL STUDIES EXPLANATION

Cultures Collide in the Americas

In this Social Studies Explanation activity, you will use a template to assemble evidence from the sources you have explored. Then, you will write an answer to the Essential Question and defend your answer with supporting evidence.

Elaborate Activities

photo: Library of Congress

INVESTIGATION TYPE: TIMELINE MAP

European Conquest of the Americas

What factors enabled Europeans to conquer all of North, Central, and South America in such a short time? Your mission is to analyze how European exploration of the Americas affected the native peoples who lived there.

PROJECTS AND ASSESSMENTS *(continued)*

photo: Getty Images

ACTIVITY TYPE: CURRENT EVENTS CONNECTION

Aztec and Modern Mexican Culture

In this activity, you will imagine you are part of a group preparing a museum exhibit comparing and contrasting ancient Aztec culture with the culture of modern Mexico. Your task is to write a newspaper article or prepare a speech publicizing the exhibit and summarizing its contents.

The Tears of the INDIANS:
BEING
An Hiſtorical and true Account
Of the Cruel
Maſſacres and Slaughters
of above Twenty Millions
of innocent People ;
Committed by the Spaniards

ACTIVITY TYPE: SAY WHAT?

Tears of the Indians

In this activity, you will translate into modern English excerpts from a 1656 English translation of Bartolomé de Las Casas's 1542 book *A Short Account of the Destruction of the Indies.*

photo: Getty Images

ACTIVITY TYPE: DOCUMENT-BASED INVESTIGATION

Cultures Collide in the Americas

In this Document-Based Investigation, you will analyze source materials and investigate this question: Is Columbus's legacy one of discovery or destruction?

Evaluate Activities

BRIEF-CONSTRUCTED RESPONSE (BCR)

Columbian Exchange

EXTENDED-CONSTRUCTED RESPONSE (ECR)

Columbian Exchange

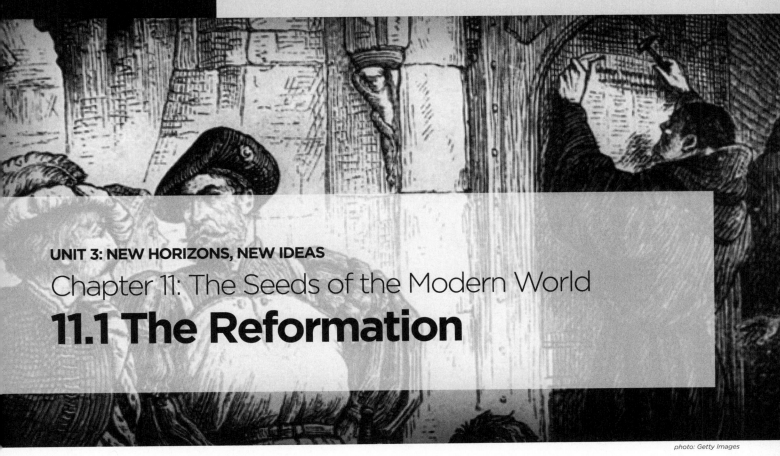

photo: Getty Images

UNIT 3: NEW HORIZONS, NEW IDEAS

Chapter 11: The Seeds of the Modern World

11.1 The Reformation

LESSON OVERVIEW

Lesson Objectives:

By the end of this lesson, you should be able to:

- Identify the causes of the upheaval of the Catholic Church.
- Trace the spread of Protestantism across Europe.
- Identify on a world map the countries and regions that remained Catholic and those that converted to Protestantism.
- Evaluate the effectiveness of the Catholic Counter-Reformation as a response to the Reformation.

Lesson Essential Question:

How did the Reformation change the balance of power in Europe?

Key Vocabulary

Calvinism, Catholic Church, England, Europe, France, heretic, indulgences, Italy, Johannes Gutenberg, John Calvin, King Ferdinand, King Henry VIII, King James Bible, Latin, Martin Luther, Muslims, New Testament, Ninety-Five Theses, parliament, pope, Protestant Church, Protestant Reformation, Protestantism, Queen Isabella, reform / social reform, Sir Thomas More, Spain, taxes, William Shakespeare, William Tyndale

DISCOVERY EDUCATION | SOCIAL STUDIES TECHBOOK

FLASHCARDS

1 Causes of the Reformation

By the early 1500s, the conditions in the Catholic Church made people begin to question its authority.

- Catholic Church leaders had become politically powerful throughout Europe.
- The Church had grown very wealthy.
- Many Church leaders were corrupt and used their offices for their own gain.
- Church leaders sold indulgences, which were pardons for sins.

Why Does It Matter?

These Church practices made many people believe that it was time for the Catholic Church to make significant changes.

photo: Library of Congress

Many people were unhappy with Church practices in the early 1500s.

2 The Spread of Protestantism

Beginning in 1517, people began publicly criticizing the Church, and new Protestant churches developed.

- Martin Luther became known as the leader of the Protestant Reformation when he posted his Ninety-Five Theses in Germany.
- After Luther's ideas spread, John Calvin founded another branch of Protestantism in Switzerland.
- In England, Henry VIII broke away from the Catholic Church and established the Church of England.

Why Does It Matter?

The actions of these leaders spread the Protestant Reformation throughout Europe.

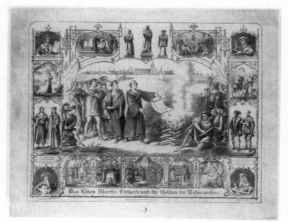

photo: Library of Congress

Martin Luther, John Calvin, and other religious and political leaders helped to spread the ideas of Protestantism.

FLASHCARDS *(continued)*

3 ## A Changing Continent

By the middle of the 1500s, Protestantism had taken hold in several parts of Europe.

- Northern Germany, the Netherlands, Scandinavia, England, and parts of Scotland became Protestant.
- Much of France, Switzerland, and Ireland and all of Italy, Spain, and Portugal remained Catholic.

Why Does It Matter?

As a result of the Reformation, the Catholic Church no longer dominated Europe, and its power was weakened.

photo: Discovery Education

After the Reformation, Protestantism was the main religion of many places in northern Europe.

4 ## The Counter-Reformation

In response to the Reformation, the Catholic Church took actions to reform and spread its faith.

- New orders, such as the Jesuits, were created to defend the Church and teach people its main tenets.
- The Council of Trent, a group of Church leaders, met to clarify their views on several issues that had led to the Reformation.
- In some countries, especially Spain, a Church court known as the Inquisition tried and punished people who it believed were heretics.

Why Does It Matter?

These actions limited the further spread of Protestantism but did not change the fact that new religions now existed and Europe would never be the same.

photo: Library of Congress

As part of the Counter-Reformation, Ignatius of Loyola founded the Jesuits to strengthen the Catholic Church. Many Jesuit priests also served as inquisitors during the Inquisition.

Name _____ **Date** _____

GRAPHIC ORGANIZER: Main Idea Web

Use this Main Idea Web to record information related to the problems facing the Catholic Church in the 1500s. For supporting resources, go to New Horizons, New Ideas > The Seeds of the Modern World > The Reformation > Explore > The Catholic Church in the 1500s.

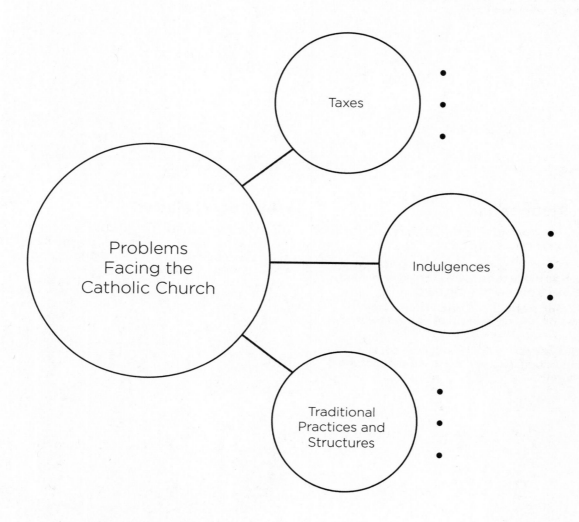

Discovery EDUCATION | SOCIAL STUDIES **TECHBOOK**

Name _____ Date _____

GRAPHIC ORGANIZER: Cause/Event/Effect Chart

Use this Cause/Event/Effect Chart to record the causes and effects of each event related to the Protestant Reformation. For supporting resources, go to New Horizons, New Ideas > The Seeds of the Modern World > The Reformation > Explore > Martin Luther.

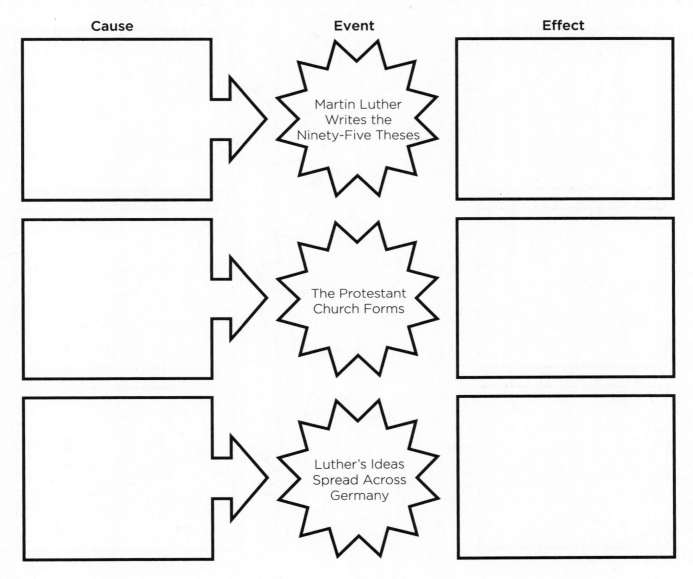

Cause | Event | Effect

Martin Luther Writes the Ninety-Five Theses

The Protestant Church Forms

Luther's Ideas Spread Across Germany

Name _____ **Date** _____

GRAPHIC ORGANIZER: Cause/Event/Effect Chart *(continued)*

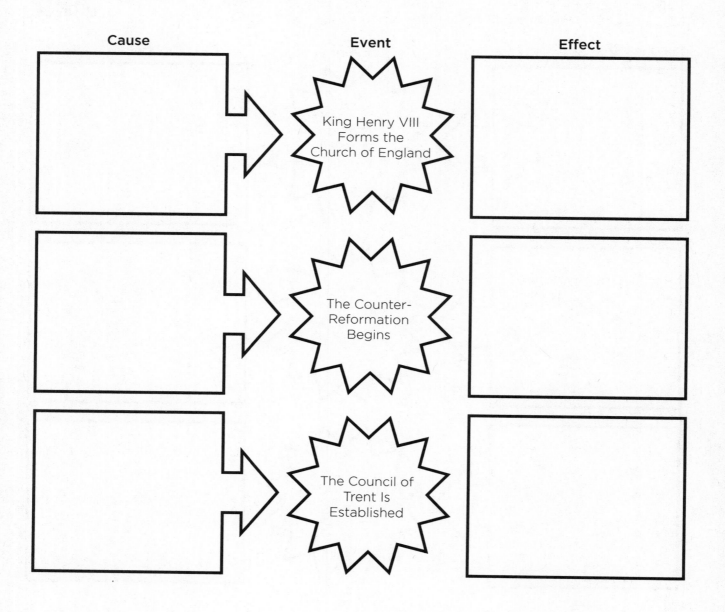

Cause	Event	Effect
	King Henry VIII Forms the Church of England	
	The Counter-Reformation Begins	
	The Council of Trent Is Established	

Name _____ **Date** _____

GRAPHIC ORGANIZER: Main Idea Web

Use this Main Idea Web to record information related to the effects of the Inquisition and the Protestant Reformation. For supporting resources, go to New Horizons, New Ideas > The Seeds of the Modern World > The Reformation > Explore > The Inquisition.

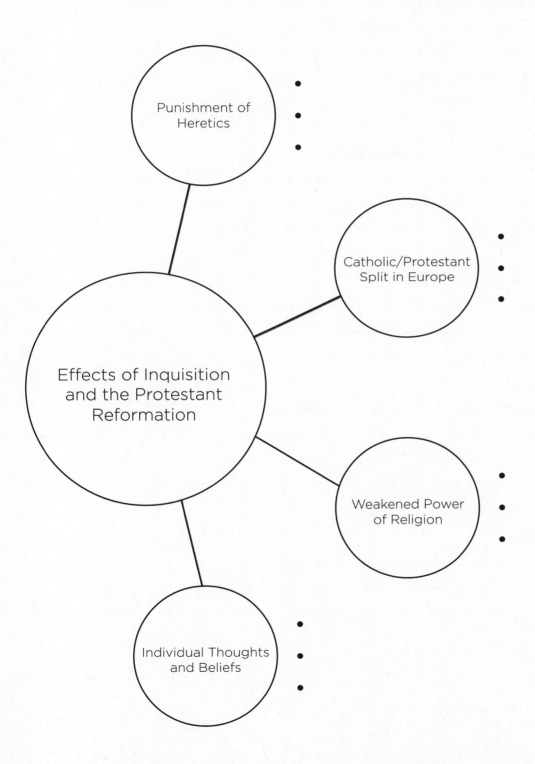

Name _____ Date _____

EXPLORE: FOCUS QUESTIONS

Using what you learned from the Core Interactive Text, answer each page's focus question:

The Catholic Church in the 1500s

What was the Catholic Church like in the early 1500s?

_____
_____
_____

Martin Luther

What role did Martin Luther play in the Reformation?

_____
_____
_____

Other Reformers

How did the Reformation spread across Europe?

_____
_____
_____

The Counter-Reformation

How did the Catholic Church respond to the Reformation?

_____
_____
_____

The Inquisition

What was the Inquisition?

_____
_____
_____

Name _____ Date _____

EXPLORE: FOCUS QUESTIONS *(continued)*

Effects of the Reformation
How did the Reformation change Europe?

_____

_____

_____

Global Religious Change
What changes to religious practice occurred outside Europe during the Reformation?

_____

_____

_____

PROJECTS AND ASSESSMENTS

Explain Activities

ACTIVITY TYPE: VISUALIZATION

The Reformation

In this activity, you will use the Cause/Event/Effect Chart you completed during the previous session to illustrate six events related to the Reformation and the Counter-Reformation.

ACTIVITY TYPE: YOU AS JOURNALIST

The Reformation

In this activity, you will interview a key figure of either the Reformation or Counter-Reformation movement and write an article describing the person's role in that movement, as well as his or her ideas, beliefs, and goals for the future.

ACTIVITY TYPE: SOCIAL STUDIES EXPLANATION

The Reformation

In this Social Studies Explanation activity, you will use a template to assemble evidence from the sources you have explored. Then, you will write an answer to the Essential Question and defend your answer with supporting evidence.

Elaborate Activities

photo: Pixabay

INVESTIGATION TYPE: HISTORICAL PERSPECTIVES

The Reformation

In this activity, you will learn about Henry VIII, William Tyndale, Queen Mary, and Elizabeth I. Based on their profiles, you will decide how each person might react to the key issues during the Protestant Reformation.

PROJECTS AND ASSESSMENTS *(continued)*

photo: Pixabay

ACTIVITY TYPE: MAKE A MODEL

Architecture and Belief

In this activity, you will draw or build a model of either a Catholic church or a Protestant church. Then, you will write a description of the church explaining how its architectural features reflect the beliefs and views of worshippers about the role of God and individuals in the church.

photo: Getty Images

ACTIVITY TYPE: SAY WHAT?

The Ninety-Five Theses

In this activity, you will translate Martin Luther's 95 theses into your own words. Next, you will write a letter to Pope Leo X advising him on how he should respond to Luther's ideas.

photo: Pixabay

ACTIVITY TYPE: DOCUMENT-BASED INVESTIGATION

The Reformation

In this Document-Based Investigation, you will analyze source materials and investigate this question: Was the spread of Protestantism in England a result of religious fervor or political convenience?

PROJECTS AND ASSESSMENTS *(continued)*

Evaluate Activities

 BRIEF-CONSTRUCTED RESPONSE (BCR)

The Reformation

 EXTENDED-CONSTRUCTED RESPONSE (ECR)

The Reformation

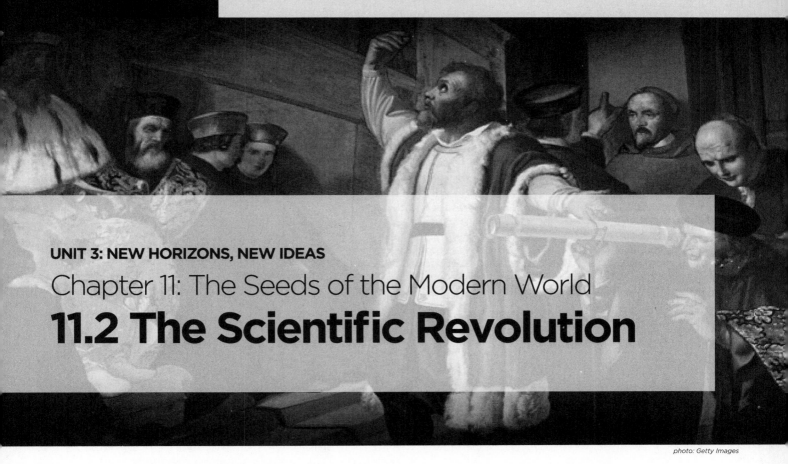

photo: Getty Images

UNIT 3: NEW HORIZONS, NEW IDEAS

Chapter 11: The Seeds of the Modern World

11.2 The Scientific Revolution

LESSON OVERVIEW

Lesson Objectives:

By the end of this lesson, you should be able to:

- Analyze the relationship between the Scientific Revolution and its predecessors, including Renaissance humanism and Greek rationalism.
- Analyze the impact of the Scientific Revolution.
- Identify important figures (e.g., Copernicus, Galileo, Kepler, and Newton) of the Scientific Revolution and their contributions.

Key Vocabulary

Amerigo Vespucci, Aristotle, Catholic Church, Francis Bacon, Galileo, heretic, humanism, Isaac Newton, Johannes Kepler, King George III, Leonardo da Vinci, Machiavelli, mercantilism, Nicolaus Copernicus, pope, Protestant Church, Renaissance, Scientific Revolution

Lesson Essential Question:

How did the Scientific Revolution change the way people understood the world?

FLASHCARDS

1 Combining Old and New

Ideas from the ancient Greeks and the Renaissance period influenced the Scientific Revolution.

- Renaissance humanism encouraged people to explore knowledge in all areas.
- With the philosophy of humanism, people asked questions and examined the world more thoroughly.
- The humanism movement began in literature and the arts but extended into other areas, including science.
- During the Renaissance, thinkers rediscovered texts and classical works by ancient Greeks. Greek rationalism stated that thinkers should use reason to discover truths about the world.

Why Does It Matter?

The thinkers of the Scientific Revolution drew upon humanism in their quest to analyze the natural world. They built upon ideas that were developed by the ancient Greeks, including Greek rationalism, to help them look at their world in a more rational, logical way and to help them seek realistic, accurate answers to questions about the universe.

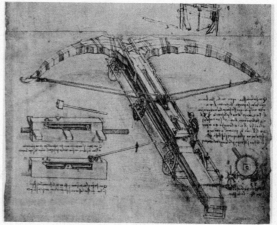

photo: Library of Congress

The Scientific Revolution was in part brought on by the developments and achievements of the Renaissance.

2 Shifting Beliefs

With the Scientific Revolution, thinkers began looking for rational, logical explanations for how the world worked. The mythical stories of the Bible were no longer the ultimate authority on the universe.

- Before the Scientific Revolution, the Bible was the ultimate authority on everything in the universe. There was no separation between religion and science.
- During the Scientific Revolution, Europeans began observing the natural world. They conducted experiments and came up with reasonable theories about how the universe operated based on the evidence they could find.
- Some of the scientific theories presented went against the teachings of the Catholic Church.
- Beliefs that went against the Church were labeled heresy. People could be jailed or killed for committing heresy.

Why Does It Matter?

The Scientific Revolution represented a major change in how people explained the world around them. They began making observations and conducting experiments to find rational, logical evidence that explained some of the mysteries of the universe. This was the basis for modern science.

photo: Library of Congress

During the Scientific Revolution, people began to challenge existing ideas and beliefs and to carefully examine the natural world.

FLASHCARDS *(continued)*

3

Scientific Minds

There were several important thinkers who developed new theories about the universe during the time of the Scientific Revolution.

- Before the Scientific Revolution, it was accepted that Earth was the center of the universe.
- Nicolaus Copernicus came up with a new model of the universe. It put the sun at the center and had Earth and the other planets orbiting the sun. This went against the common beliefs of the day.
- Copernicus's model formed the basis for what we now know about planetary motion. It helped spur the work of later scientists.
- Johannes Kepler added to Copernicus's model by showing that the planets orbited the sun in ellipses, or oval orbits, and not circles.
- Galileo was the first known person to study the sky with a telescope. He observed that the surface of the moon is not smooth and that Jupiter has several moons that orbit it.
- Galileo's observations confirmed Copernicus's model of the universe. The Catholic Church put Galileo on trial for his beliefs. He was charged as a heretic and imprisoned under house arrest.
- Isaac Newton was one of the later and most important scientists of the Scientific Revolution.
- Newton discovered the principles of gravity at work on Earth and in the universe.
- Newton developed the universal law of gravity. He also discovered the three laws of motion.
- Newton's discoveries are the basis of modern physics.

Why Does It Matter?

The scientific thinkers of the Scientific Revolution built on one another's work and expanded their new theories to form the backbone of what we now believe to be true about our universe. Without Copernicus, the others may not have made the discoveries that they did. Finally, Newton put everyone's ideas together by offering a complete picture of planetary motion and developing the laws of motion that govern modern physics today.

photo: Discovery Education

Newton was born in 1643 and died in 1727. He was one of the most important thinkers of the Scientific Revolution.

Name _____ Date _____

GRAPHIC ORGANIZER: Change Over Time Chart

Use this Change Over Time Chart to record information about the changes that took place during the Scientific Revolution. For supporting resources, go to New Horizons, New Ideas > The Seeds of the Modern World > The Scientific Revolution > Explore > The Influence of the Renaissance.

Before:	After:

Changes:

Name _____ **Date** _____

GRAPHIC ORGANIZER: Sequencing Chart

Complete this Sequencing Chart by listing in chronological order and summarizing the importance of the major discoveries and innovations of the Scientific Revolution. For supporting resources, go to New Horizons, New Ideas > The Seeds of the Modern World > The Scientific Revolution > Explore > A New Theory on the Cosmos.

Event	Date	Summary

Name _____**Date** _____

GRAPHIC ORGANIZER: Sequencing Chart *(continued)*

Event	Date	Summary

Name _____ Date _____

EXPLORE: FOCUS QUESTIONS

Using what you learned from the Core Interactive Text, answer each page's focus question:

The Influence of the Renaissance
How did the Renaissance lead to the Scientific Revolution?

_____

_____

_____

Revolutionary Influences
What role did ancient Greek philosophers play in the Scientific Revolution?

_____

_____

_____

A New Way of Thinking
How did the Scientific Revolution change the way Europeans explained the world?

_____

_____

_____

A New Theory on the Cosmos
Who was Nicolaus Copernicus?

_____

_____

_____

Copernicus's New Theory
How did Copernicus change astronomy?

_____

_____

_____

An Elliptical Orbit
How did Johannes Kepler expand upon Copernicus's work?

_____

_____

_____

Name _____ Date _____

EXPLORE: FOCUS QUESTIONS *(continued)*

Galileo's Fight
How did Galileo confirm Copernicus's theories about the planets?

 _____
_____
_____

Newton and Gravity
What scientific contributions did Isaac Newton make?

_____
_____
_____

Explaining the Laws of Motion
What did Newton discover about the way objects move?

_____
_____
_____

PROJECTS AND ASSESSMENTS

Explain Activities

ACTIVITY TYPE: DIAGRAM

The Scientific Revolution

In this activity, you will design a graphic organizer that shows the relationships among people, events, and ideas during the Scientific Revolution.

ACTIVITY TYPE: MOVIE TRAILER

The Scientific Revolution

In this activity, you will create a movie trailer for a new movie that uncovers the story behind the Scientific Revolution.

ACTIVITY TYPE: QUICK WRITE

The Scientific Revolution

In this activity, you will write a response that explores the effects of the scientific revolution on the world.

ACTIVITY TYPE: SOCIAL STUDIES EXPLANATION

The Scientific Revolution

In this Social Studies Explanation activity, you will use a template to assemble evidence from the sources you have explored. Then, you will write an answer to the Essential Question and defend your answer with supporting evidence.

Elaborate Activities

photo: Library of Congress

INVESTIGATION TYPE: TIMELINE INQUIRY

The Scientific Revolution

Your mission is to learn how early modern scientists shifted their study of math, biology, and the universe from a religious focus to the objective study of nature. How did the leaders of the Scientific Revolution give people a new way to understand the world?

PROJECTS AND ASSESSMENTS *(continued)*

photo: From The New York Public Library

ACTIVITY TYPE: PITCH YOUR IDEA

A Scientific Ride

In this activity, you will create a proposal for building a roller coaster ride and present your plan to a wealthy landowner.

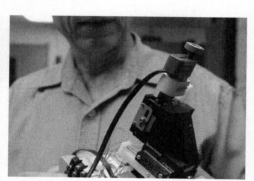

ACTIVITY TYPE: CURRENT EVENTS CONNECTION

Discovering Mars

In this activity, you will research both the earliest and the most recent scientific discoveries about Mars and how they were made. You will then write an illustrated introduction to your exhibit that shows how the changes in thinking that took place during the 1500s and 1600s made our modern research possible.

photo: Library of Congresss

ACTIVITY TYPE: DOCUMENT-BASED INVESTIGATION

The Scientific Revolution

In this Document-Based Investigation, you will analyze source materials and investigate this question: To what extent were the theories of the Scientific Revolution incompatible with religious teachings of the time?

Evaluate Activities

BRIEF-CONSTRUCTED RESPONSE (BCR)

The Scientific Revolution

EXTENDED-CONSTRUCTED RESPONSE (ECR)

The Scientific Revolution

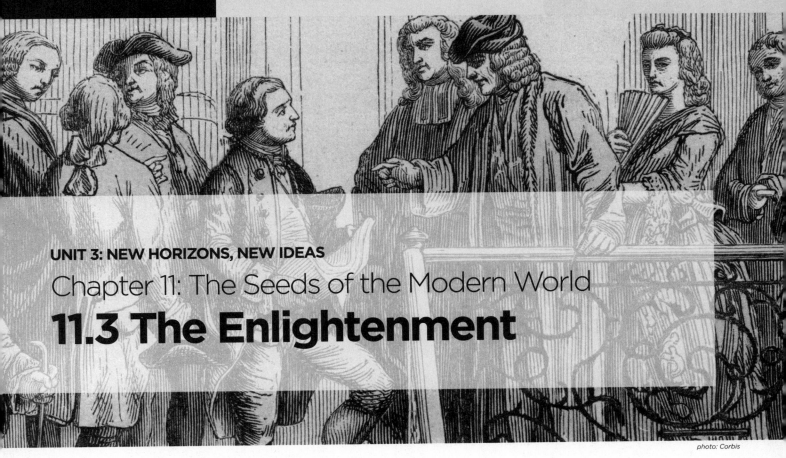

photo: Corbis

UNIT 3: NEW HORIZONS, NEW IDEAS

Chapter 11: The Seeds of the Modern World

11.3 The Enlightenment

LESSON OVERVIEW

Lesson Objectives:

By the end of this lesson, you should be able to:

- Analyze the relationship between the Enlightenment and its predecessors including the Renaissance, Roman republicanism, and the Scientific Revolution.

- Analyze the impact of the Enlightenment on thought, reason, and society.

- Identify important Enlightenment thinkers (Diderot, Kant, Locke, Montesquieu, and Voltaire) and their contributions.

Lesson Essential Question:

How did the philosophies of the Enlightenment influence politics and society in Europe?

Key Vocabulary

autonomy, Baron de Montesquieu, Declaration of the Rights of Man and of the Citizen, democracy, Denis Diderot, Enlightenment, Francis Bacon, Frederick II, Galileo, humanism, Immanuel Kant, individualism, Jean-Jacques Rousseau, John Locke, King George III, laissez-faire, Nicolaus Copernicus, parliament, philosophy, Rationalism, Renaissance, republicanism, Scientific Revolution, social contract, Thomas Hobbes, unicameral, Voltaire

FLASHCARDS

1 ▸ Ideas That Led to the Enlightenment

The Enlightenment, an intellectual movement that occurred in the 1600s and 1700s, had its roots in earlier trends and ideas.

- The Scientific Revolution gave people faith that they could use reason to understand the world around them.
- Humanism, a philosophy that gained influence during the Renaissance, made thinkers value human life and achievements more than they had previously.
- Enlightenment thinkers admired the democratic elements of the ancient Greek and Roman governments.

Why Does It Matter?

Enlightenment thinkers applied the ideas of these earlier movements to develop new ideas and theories about human society.

photo: Byrd, Robert C. The Senate of the Roman Republic: Addresses on the History of Roman Constitutionalism. Washington, DC: U.S. Government Printing Office, 1995.
The thinkers of the Enlightenment used ideas of science and of ancient Greece and Rome to develop new theories of how the world worked.

2 ▸ *Philosophes* and Other Enlightenment Thinkers

Philosophers from across Europe shared and contributed ideas to the Enlightenment.

- John Locke, a British philosopher, wrote about human nature and said that people were born with natural rights such as life, liberty, and property.
- Voltaire, Jean-Jacques Rousseau, and the Baron de Montesquieu lived in Paris and wrote about society and governments that respected people's rights. Denis Diderot collected the ideas of the *philosophes* in a multivolume *Encyclopédie*.
- Immanuel Kant, a German philosopher, wrote that people should use rational thought when making moral decisions.

Why Does It Matter?

By writing and sharing their ideas, these philosophers changed the way people thought about government and people's rights.

photo: Library of Congress
John Locke, the Baron de Montesquieu, and Voltaire were all influential political thinkers during the Enlightenment.

FLASHCARDS *(continued)*

3 ▶ ### The Impact of the Enlightenment

In the 1700s, some political leaders adopted Enlightenment ideas as the basis for their governments.

- Enlightened despots, such as Frederick II of Prussia, created some reforms based on new ideas but did not create significant changes.
- The leaders of the American Revolution adopted Enlightenment ideas such as inalienable rights and the separation of powers in the Declaration of Independence and the U.S. Constitution.
- The leaders of the French Revolution used the ideas of natural rights and a social contract when they overthrew their government and wrote the Declaration of the Rights of Man and of the Citizen.

Why Does It Matter?

The political ideas developed during the Enlightenment changed several governments at the time and became the basis for the way many people today think about government and human rights.

photo: Library of Congress

The ideas of the Enlightenment had a direct effect on the leaders of the American and French Revolutions.

Name _____ Date _____

GRAPHIC ORGANIZER: Cause/Event/Effect Chart

Use this Cause/Event/Effect Chart to record the causes and effects related to each of the events listed in the starbursts. For supporting resources, go to New Horizons, New Ideas > The Seeds of the Modern World > The Enlightenment > Explore > The Roots of the Enlightenment.

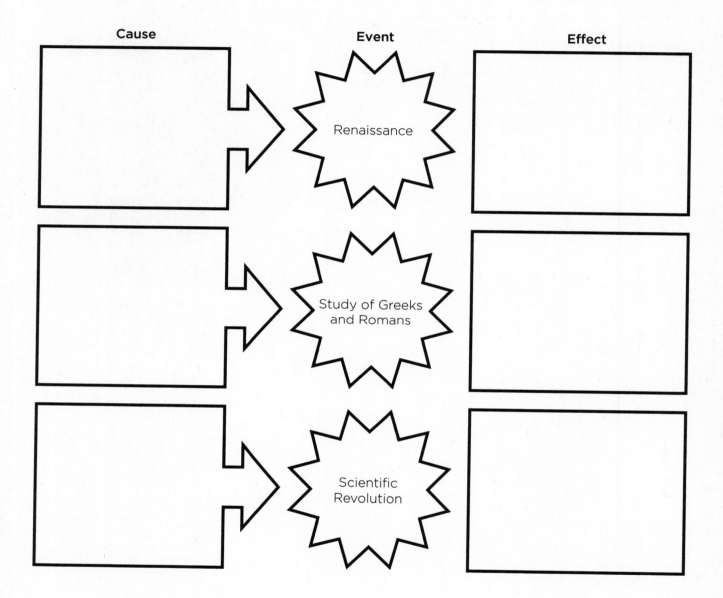

Cause | Event | Effect

Renaissance

Study of Greeks and Romans

Scientific Revolution

SOCIAL STUDIES
TECHBOOK

Name _____**Date** _____

GRAPHIC ORGANIZER: Main Idea Web

Use this Main Idea Web to record information about the three basic principles of the Enlightenment. For supporting resources, go to New Horizons, New Ideas > The Seeds of the Modern World > The Enlightenment > Explore > Fundamental Ideas.

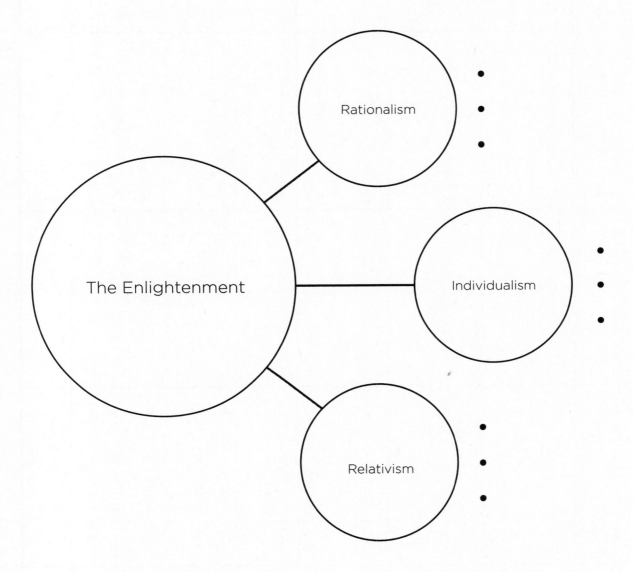

Name _____ Date _____

GRAPHIC ORGANIZER: Comparison Chart

Use this Comparison Chart to identify similarities and differences among the Enlightenment thinkers. For supporting resources, go to New Horizons, New Ideas > The Seeds of the Modern World > The Enlightenment > Explore > Locke and Hobbes.

Thinker	Background	Main Ideas About Government
Hobbes		
Locke		
Voltaire		
Montesquieu		

Name _____**Date** _____

GRAPHIC ORGANIZER: Comparison Chart *(continued)*

Thinker	Background	Main Ideas About Government
Rousseau		
Diderot		
Kant		

Name _____ **Date** _____

GRAPHIC ORGANIZER: Main Idea Web

Use this Main Idea Web to record information about the people and movements that were influenced by the Enlightenment. For supporting resources, go to New Horizons, New Ideas > The Seeds of the Modern World > The Enlightenment > Explore > Influence of the Enlightenment.

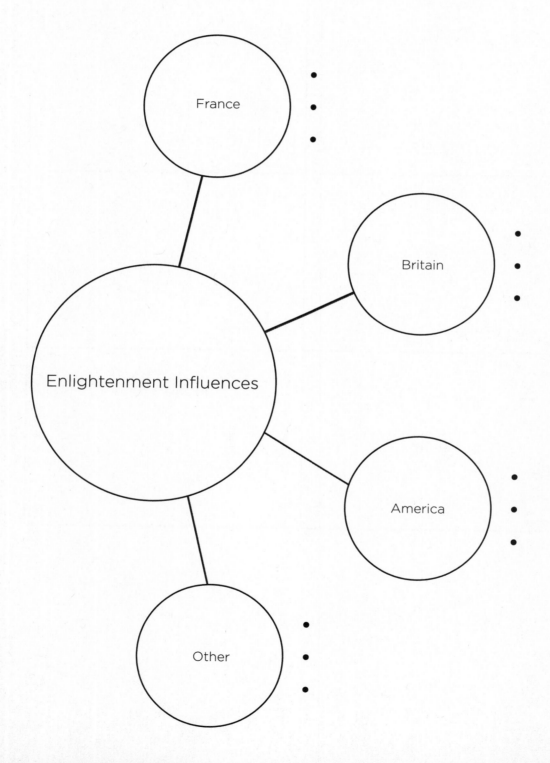

Name _____ Date _____

EXPLORE: FOCUS QUESTIONS

Using what you learned from the Core Interactive Text, answer each page's focus question:

The Roots of the Enlightenment
Where did Enlightenment ideas come from?

_____

_____

_____

Fundamental Ideas
What were the fundamental concepts of the Enlightenment?

_____

_____

_____

Locke and Hobbes
Who were John Locke and Thomas Hobbes?

_____

_____

_____

The Enlightenment in France and Germany
Who were some of the other important thinkers of the Enlightenment?

_____

_____

_____

Rousseau and Diderot
What were the contributions of Rousseau and Diderot?

_____

_____

_____

The Influence of the Enlightenment
How did Enlightenment thinkers affect society and government in Europe and America?

_____

_____

_____

Name _____ Date _____

EXPLORE: FOCUS QUESTIONS *(continued)*

The Enlightenment Spreads
What role did Enlightenment ideas play in the American Revolution?

_____
_____
_____

Revolution Spreads
What role did Enlightenment ideas play in the French Revolution?

_____
_____
_____

PROJECTS AND ASSESSMENTS

Explain Activities

ACTIVITY TYPE: ENCYCLOPEDIA ENTRY

Enlightenment Thinkers

In this activity, you will create an encyclopedia entry for an important Enlightenment thinker.

ACTIVITY TYPE: QUICK WRITE

Enlightenment Thinking

In this Quick Write, you will take the perspective of a member of the clergy in France in the 1770s, a colonist in America who opposes British policies in the 1770s, or a member of Parliament in Great Britain in the 1770s. You will then write a short essay on the importance of the Enlightenment on government and society.

ACTIVITY TYPE: SOCIAL STUDIES EXPLANATION

The Enlightenment

In this Social Studies Explanation activity, you will use a template to assemble evidence from the sources you have explored. Then, you will write an answer to the Essential Question and defend your answer with supporting evidence.

Elaborate Activities

photo: Getty Images

INVESTIGATION TYPE: ENDURING DEBATE

Locke vs. Hobbes

What is the role of the individual in society?

photo: Getty Images

ACTIVITY TYPE: ROLE PLAY

Government and the Enlightenment

In this activity, you will take part in a conversation between a government leader and an influential Enlightenment philosopher.

PROJECTS AND ASSESSMENTS *(continued)*

photo: Library of Congress

ACTIVITY TYPE: SAY WHAT?

Rousseau and Government

In this activity, you will translate an excerpt from Jean-Jacques Rousseau's "*The Social Contract*."

photo: Library of Congress

ACTIVITY TYPE: DOCUMENT-BASED INVESTIGATION

The Enlightenment

In this Document-Based Investigation, you will analyze source materials and investigate this question: To what extent did the French and American revolutions fulfill Enlightenment ideals? Which revolution best represented these ideals?

Evaluate Activities

BRIEF-CONSTRUCTED RESPONSE (BCR)

Principles of the Enlightenment

EXTENDED-CONSTRUCTED RESPONSE (ECR)

Principles of the Enlightenment